PRAISE FOR
1,001 WAYS TO KEEP CUSTOMERS COMING BACK

"Wow, indeed! If your goal is to be customer centric, then this is the book to read!"

—LYNN DENSFORD, editor of *Corporate University Review*

"This book has never failed to point me in the right direction: keeping the customer satisfied. It's not a book, it's a salesperson's Bible."

—SAM ALFSTAD, editor of *eMarketer.com*

"It's expensive finding—and losing—new customers. If you want to get off that merry-go-round, this is the book for you."

—CHRIS LEE, managing editor of *Training*

"A compendium of the most advanced customer retention techniques. . . . I highly recommend it."

—HOMER HEWITT, CEO of VideoLearning

"Read it again and again—every time you want to boost your ability to please the people you need most: your customers."

—TOM BROWN, Management General

1,001 WAYS TO KEEP CUSTOMERS COMING BACK

1,001 Ways to Keep Customers Coming Back

Wow Ideas That Make Customers Happy and Will Increase Your Bottom Line

Donna Greiner
Theodore B. Kinni

Prima Publishing

Library of Congress Cataloging-in-Publication Data
Greiner, Donna.
    1,001 ways to keep customers coming back : wow ideas that make customers happy and will increase your bottom line. Donna Greiner and Theodore B. Kinni.
        p.   cm.
    Includes index.
    ISBN 0-7615-2029-5
    1. Consumer satisfaction. 2. Customer services. 3. Customer relations.
    4. Customer loyalty. I. Kinni, Theodore B. II. Title. III. Title: One thousand one ways to keep customers coming back. IV. Title: One thousand and one ways to keep customers coming back.
HF5415.335.G74   1999
658.8'12—dc21   99-16904
                                                                                          CIP

99 00 01 02 HH 10 9 8 7 6 5 4 3 2 1
Printed in the United States of America

How to Order
Single copies may be ordered from Prima Publishing, P.O. Box 1260BK, Rocklin, CA 95677; telephone (916) 632-4400. Quantity discounts are also available. On your letterhead, include information concerning the intended use of the books and the number of books you wish to purchase.

Visit us online at www.primalifestyles.com

CONTENTS

FOREWORD

There's only one idea in this entire book.

Fortunately for you, it's a great idea. An idea that will make your small business bigger or your big business more profitable. An idea that's been overlooked by most marketers, and one that doesn't require an awful lot of investment, machinery, or risk. The fact is that most companies are obsessed with getting new customers. They advertise, plead, cajole, bribe and bend over backwards to get a new customer. And then, once they get them, treat them like dirt. Wish that they'd go away. Disrespect them. Cease to invest. In general, marketers act like idiots when it comes to great customers.

And this book will open your eyes to the problem and give you not ten, not twenty, but literally one thousand ways to do something about it.

Let me tell you a story. United Airlines found a great customer when they found me. I fly nearly 100,000 miles a year on United, and often fly full fare or business class because of my speaking schedule. People like me account for less than 20% of United's passenger load and more than 80% of their profits.

On a recent transatlantic flight, I paid a whole bunch of money for a round trip. And the service was terrible. The seats were broken, the cabin was filthy, the food was awful— even for airline food. So I wrote a letter. I calmly described how disappointed I was. And sure enough, a few days letter, I got a response. You know what they sent me?

A form letter that said they appreciated hearing about how horrible the flight was. And coupons (with a full page of rules) worth about 4% of what I paid for the flight.

The same day that they spent a hundred bucks to keep a super-great customer, how much do you think they spent in a vain quest to find a new customer to take my place? How many TV ads, billboards, promotional giveaways and discounted fares do you think it will take them to find someone who will switch to United and fly 75,000 full-fare miles next year?

Sure, it's common sense. Invest time and money to keep your best customers happy, spend less replacing them. Common sense, unfortunately, isn't that common. So here's your chance. Go ahead and decimate the competition. Figure out how to keep people coming back and win.

Have fun!

—Seth Godin, author of *Permission Marketing*
and coauthor of *The Guerrilla Marketing Handbook*

ACKNOWLEDGMENTS

First, we'd like to thank all of the companies and professionals featured in the following pages for providing so many great examples and so much expert thinking. As businesspeople, we appreciate your help in making our company better at keeping customers; as customers, we appreciate the value you place on our patronage.

Second, we are grateful to everyone who helped us find so many creative ideas. They told us with which companies they like to do business and why; they also freely shared their personal experiences. Thanks to all of you—in particular, Frank Cumiskey, Pam and Jeff Hegedus, the Tim Kinni family, Ken and Shirley Lyon, and Lois Snyder.

Finally, thanks as always to super agent John Willig, who so wisely judges our book ideas and unfailingly finds the right publishers for them.

INTRODUCTION

Keep Them Coming Back

There is a saying in China: "To open a business is very easy; to keep it open is very difficult." This book is aimed at keeping a business open, or more accurately, keeping the customers who support the business coming back.

If you are searching for ideas to build repeat business, expert thinking on the subject, or a look at the companies that are best at that task, you've come to the right place. There are 1,001 proven ideas, techniques, programs, strategies, facts, and quotes for building business with existing customers in the chapters that follow.

The 1,001 ways come from around the globe, from big and small businesses in big and small markets in just about every industry you can imagine, as well as governmental and non-profit institutions. And yet, there is really no need to search out the strategies that come from companies just like yours.

In fact, the best ideas for you may well be from a wholly unrelated business. They will be ideas that are just waiting for you to put them to work in your company, for those new twists or small tweaks that will make your business perfect for your customers.

Discount brokerage Charles Schwab & Company president David Pottruck found that out when his company focused on customers. "We pay close attention to the Wal-Marts, Home Depots, Intels, and Microsofts," he said. Those companies offered the ideas that helped Schwab attract and keep roughly half of all customers in the U.S. discount brokerage market.

The 1,001 ways include a wide geographic diversity. They come from companies in Europe, Asia, South America, and North America. They come from companies dealing with customer bases that are international, national, regional, urban, suburban, and small-town.

We also included ideas we found here in Williamsburg, Virginia. As a business market, Williamsburg is fascinating. It is a small town, a college town, and a resort town all wrapped up in one. There are the residents who comprise the year-round customers, the students who are regular seasonal customers, and the tourists who can double the population on a summer weekend and return on irregular schedules. Accordingly, the businesses here use a wide diversity of retention techniques to prosper throughout the year.

Further, Williamsburg is the home of the Colonial Williamsburg Foundation, a preeminent nonprofit that attracts around a million visitors a year, many of whom are repeat customers. Its customer and donor programs are world class, and we include several of them in this book.

How can you use the 1,001 ideas that follow? Think about how you might recreate them in a scale that fits your business, how they would work with your product or service, or how they could be applied in a different medium and a different industry. The answers to those queries will turn these ideas into another 1,001, and after that, 1,001 more.

We collected the ideas in this book over the last half of the 1990s, but did not try to impose any order on them until we started the book itself. When we finally began sorting them, we found that they fell into categories on their own. Those categories ended up covering the entire gamut of customer retention ideas and also created the organizational structure of the book.

Here is an overview of that structure and an advance look at what you will find ahead:

We start, in Chapter 1, by looking at how companies keep customers and build business with them by creating unique bundles of product and services. The best companies tailor these to fulfill a whole list of their customers' needs without forcing them to do business elsewhere.

In Chapter 2, we jump into the wide world of incentives, showing how companies use them to drive repeat business. The chapter details the use of free offers, value-added bonuses, coupons and rebates, sales, special financing, and a perennial favorite—contests.

Chapter 3 covers communities of interest—that is, creating and catering to groups of like-minded customers. Although there have always been communities of interest, the concept is just beginning to capture the attention of companies, and the consultants and academics that serve them, in a big way. Expect to hear a lot more about this in the future.

Chapter 4 examines guarantees and how they help convince customers to trust you with their repeat business. We look at examples of price, product, and service guarantees and how companies design and manage them.

Chapter 5 is the most uplifting in the book and a joy to research. It examines how companies do good and do well at the same time. The range of corporate philanthropy is wonderfully diverse and generous, as is the response from customers.

In Chapter 6, we look at how companies turn a single sale into a loyal customer by offering rewards. It starts with the basics of customer care, including getting personal with customers. This chapter presents ways to turn one sale into a second and continues with a free-ranging romp through the world of frequent buyer programs. The chapter concludes by showing how a few companies are capturing customers for life by buying back the goods they sold to them in the first place.

Chapter 7 is devoted to trophy customers—those who reside among the 20% of customers that provide 80% of your sales. It looks at how companies court their very best customers with recognition and gifts, rewards for high volume, and elite programs designed to pay off in kind.

In Chapter 8, we explore how companies create loyal customers in a hectic world by making their work and personal lives easier. Simplification and convenience are the two keys here, and there are plenty of ideas for both.

Chapter 9 covers how companies build repeat business by going to their customers. It examines how they tell customers when it is time for them to buy again. It also looks at how they keep customers coming back by not making them come back at all. Instead, the company goes to the customer.

How to keep them coming back by giving them what they want is the topic of Chapter 10. In it, we learn how companies build business by listening to customers and how they turn customer problems and complaints into future sales. It also surveys the current state of innovation, examining the products and services that result from listening to customers. And finally, the chapter turns to the cutting edge of customer retention—mass customization, the large-scale production of custom products for individual customers.

We close the book in Chapter 11 by looking at how companies earn reputations as customer service champions. We explore how such companies are led and how they are structured. And we end the chapter by celebrating customer service excellence and offering ideas for how you can, too.

Two final comments:

First, with so many companies, products, and programs, it would have been very distracting to interrupt the text with trademarks and other proprietary symbols. The reader should assume that all capitalized names are the property of their companies.

Second, you won't find negative examples here. Don't put your energy and resources into avoiding problems. If, instead, you put them into creating customers who are excited about doing business with you, most common problems will never appear.

1,001 WAYS TO KEEP CUSTOMERS COMING BACK

CREATE A BETTER BUNDLE

Bundling is the act of building an added-value package around the products and services you sell. When you offer customers a bundle, you are giving them more reasons to come back to do business with your company. Every time a customer uses and is satisfied with one of the benefits in the bundle, he or she comes another step closer to becoming a customer for life.

As we quickly found out, the possibilities of bundling are limitless. Obvious bundles include packages of products and services that naturally go together—accounting software and preprinted invoices, for instance. But, there is no reason to feel constrained by direct links. As you will soon see, just about everything can be combined in one way or another to create a bundle (how about stock trading and air travel?) that makes customers happy.

Bundles can be the simple, yet convenient addition of a small service that complements your product. Perhaps you sell postage stamps at your card shop. Or, they can entail the establishment of a series of complex partnerships between leading producers of products and services—for example, a credit card company and almost all the major airlines teaming up to offer air miles for purchases of all kinds.

Also, creating your bundle needn't increase your costs. There is no reason why you shouldn't make money on the services and products you add for your customers' convenience. The key, however, is to focus on what adds value from the customers' perspective *before* you start thinking about how much money you will make.

In any case, the final goal of bundling is always the same: to increase the reasons why your customers should return to you when they are ready to buy again. And, here are some great ideas how:

---●---

With almost 400 country store/restaurants in 30-odd states, **Cracker Barrel Old Country Stores** has built a billion-dollar business catering to highway travelers. One of the chain's best ideas for bringing travelers who are just passing through back into one of their locations involves audio books. Buy any one of the 200-plus audio books on display in one Cracker Barrel Old Country Store, listen to it on the road, and when you're done, simply drop it off at any other Cracker Barrel and collect a refund of the entire purchase price, minus a $3 rental fee.

---●---

Maryland-based **Trak Auto Corporation** is driving growth at its $300 million auto parts chain by adding the information customers need to its bundle. Its stores offer free access to Mitchell On-Demand, a computerized system packed with information on parts and how-to instructions for repairs. Customers who prefer the books to keyboards get free, unlimited access to the store's shelved Reference Library.

---●---

Customers keep coming back to Los Angeles' **Paramount Car Wash** because they don't get rubbed the wrong way. While their car is washed, customers can get a five-minute Shiatsu/ Swedish massage for only 75¢ in one of their fabulous massage chairs.

———— ● ————

Our local **Nottingham Hallmark** store provides the typical huge selection of greeting cards and gifts for every occasion. But recently, the store went a step further, providing postage stamps and a daily mail pickup for customers. It's a simple and complete bundle: Buy a card *and* a stamp, personalize it, and mail it without leaving the store. Here in Williamsburg, where the long lines at the post office are the stuff from which legends are made, this simple added service is a real loyalty builder.

———— ● ————

Delaware's **Dover Downs** racetrack expanded its appeal in and out of season by adding slot machines to its bundle. Throw in the Dover Downs Slots Capital Club, which offers members a chance to earn points redeemable for free gasoline to help defray their traveling costs to the track, and you've got a front runner.

———— ● ————

World's leading software maker **Microsoft Corporation** creates bundles that keep customers coming back so regularly that some people figure it's got to be illegal. The company landed in hot water for its Windows and Internet Explorer software bundle. Another notable Microsoft bundle is the Office suite that includes leading word processing, spreadsheet, database, and presentation software in one neat package.

———— ● ————

Another natural bundle in the software industry is software and the support so many

> If a man goes into business with only the idea of making money, the chances are he won't.
>
> —Joyce Clyde Hall, founder of Hallmark Cards, Inc.

Managers from companies in reciprocal industries should be plotting common approaches to customers through relational databases, not plotting how to take each other over.

—BENN KONSYNSKI,
EMORY UNIVERSITY PROFESSOR

customers need to make it work. **Intuit, Inc.'s** popular small business program QuickBooks keeps customers coming back with its Quick-Books Support Network plans. The Gold Plan, at $99 per year, includes five telephone sessions with QuickBooks experts and is available during extended hours. The Platinum Plan, at a cost of $189 per year, includes 10 sessions, a QuickBooks Learning Guide, and a 10% discount off QuickBooks printed supplies.

———————•———————

At a time when everyone seems to be playing the stock market in one way or another, **American Airlines** found a way to bundle stock trades and air travel to keep customers coming back. Customers trading with discount brokerage firm Bull & Bear Securities also earn American's AAdvantage frequent-flyer miles. Customers trading stocks, bonds, and options earn 500 air miles for each of their first five trades at Bull & Bear. After that, investors get 100 miles for every trade, up to 35,000 miles in any 12-month period.

———————•———————

Cars and credit cards make another good bundle. The **General Motors Corp.,** the world's biggest automaker, created the GM Master-Card. Every time you use your GM Card, 5% of the purchases accumulates toward the purchase or lease of a new GM vehicle. Each year for seven years, cardholders can earn up to $500 toward the purchase for a total of $3,500. That's a welcome bite out of the high cost of buying a new car.

———————•———————

On its home soil, German car maker **Porsche** partnered with MasterCard to create the Porsche Card. The $100 annual fee includes perks such as free parking and cleaning on AVIS' airport lots, reservation services for hotels, car rentals, restaurants, sporting events, air travel, and emergency roadside assistance. Those cardholders who combine the Porsche with the Lufthansa AirPlus VISA also receive priority for standby travel and use of airport clubs.

————•————

DaimlerChrysler created its bundle for Mercedes owners in Germany around the Mercedes Card, which comes with or without a credit card feature. Cardholders receive a bonus bundle that includes a bimonthly newsletter, annual calendar, movie premiere tickets, invitations to Mercedes special events, along with exclusive vacation offers.

————•————

Bundling can be the key to turning a mundane service into something with more zing. There are few places as boring as the typical Laundromat, where the deadly hum of washers and dryers can numb even the most alert mind—except at San Francisco's **Brain Wash.** There customers can fire up the washers and step into the café for a specialty coffee and a snack while enjoying live music and poetry readings. Chicago-based **Rock & Fold** puts another spin on the same business by adding five movie screens and piped-in gospel music.

————•————

The **Art Bar** in Philadelphia got nationwide press when it debuted its unique bundle in 1998. Owner David Simons gave artists a free alternative to formal classes by giving them a place to buy a beer and draw a nude at the same time. In a bid to earn the patronage and loyalty of artsy customers, the Art Bar supplies the models, hosts poetry readings, plays alternative music, and sells beer for $1.50 a bottle.

You don't need to be in the entertainment business to make your business more entertaining. The idea is to make your place of business fun to visit, a place where your customers can feel good.

—JOE VITALE IN
*THERE'S A CUSTOMER BORN
EVERY MINUTE*

————— ● —————

In an industry dominated by huge companies, such as Dell and Compaq, you might think that a small, local company would have a hard time competing. Not so, at **College & University Computers, Inc.** (CUC), which bills itself as "Williamsburg's *Super* Computer Store" and recently made the *Inc.* 500 list of fastest-growing small companies. Understanding that computer buyers often need instruction, CUC teamed up with Virginia's Thomas Nelson Community College to open a Computer Training Center just two doors away from its retail store. CUC provides the space and the equipment, and the community college provides the instructors and administration for courses in popular software, the Internet, and group training for businesses.

————— ● —————

The bundling of banks and supermarkets is pretty commonplace these days and most chain food stores contain a bank branch, but **First Market Bank of Virginia,** which operates inside the Richmond-based Ukrop's Super Markets, Inc. grocery chain, is unique. The bank itself was created to add to the Ukrop's service bundle. It is a joint venture between the supermarket chain, which owns 51% of First Market, and National Commerce Bancorporation—the first bank to ever be owned by its host store.

First Market builds repeat business for itself and the supermarket with its Market Share Program. The plan awards points based on every $25 spent at Ukrop's and every $100 in average quarterly balances in First Market accounts, in addition to points for other bank services. Points are redeemed in grocery discounts and up to $200 a year in gift certificates for free groceries.

———— • ————

Ukrop's also builds repeat business for its in-store pharmacy by adding medical services, in the form of health screenings, to its product bundle. The chain schedules a new screening each month covering simple diagnostic testing for high blood pressure, diabetes, and cholesterol, and commonly needed vaccines, such as flu shots. The events are co-sponsored by area health industry partners and customers get them free or at a very small charge.

———— • ————

Target Stores, Inc. offers the same service with a twist: It bundles them into free Medical Fairs and invites anyone in the community to attend. A recent fair included diabetes and cholesterol checks, blood work, hearing tests, and free consultations with a chiropractor and a dentist. The services run concurrently on a Saturday.

———— • ————

Small business **Berkeley Pharmacy** made simple, low-cost and free health services a permanent part of its business. A wellness center inside the store offers five health-screening procedures, including tests of bone density, lipid profiles, cardiovascular disease, and body composition, including body fat analysis and facial skin condition.

———— • ————

Dr. Patricia Deckert, an Alpine, California-based osteopath, turned the above idea on its head by expanding her medical service to include products. She added a "lifestyle educator," who advises patients on diet, exercise, and spiritual well-being, to her staff and sells products such as vitamins, nutritional supplements, and natural medicines. The sale of the products offsets the lifestyle educator's salary, and customers get valuable guidance and convenience when buying supplements.

———— • ————

Shaia Oriental Rugs made sure its customers kept it in mind by adding cleaning and repair services to its inventory of new and antique rugs. The service helps protect the customers' investments, keeps them coming back to the store, and further establishes the company's expert reputation.

———— • ————

The nation's leading bookseller **Barnes & Noble, Inc.** makes much of its $2.8 billion in annual revenues in its superstores, a bundle that transformed the industry in the early 1990s. Suddenly, bookstores featured a staggering selection of books and magazines; cafés serving coffee, soft drinks, snacks, and sweets; music; and steep discounts. They became destinations in and of themselves, even for less-than-avid readers.

———— • ————

Follett Corporation is testing the superstore concept for its over 500 college bookstores at its University of Illinois location. The store offers Internet stations with free access, on-demand publishing, music, books, software, a "cyberwall" featuring sports and educational programming, and electronic message boards. And, in the midst of all of this is a café serving tasty fare including fruit smoothies and sandwiches.

———— • ————

The nation's independent bookstores are fighting back with bundles of their own: **Cyrano's Bookstore, Café, Cinema & Off-Center Playhouse** in Anchorage, Alaska, thinks of itself as a "cultural mini-mall." The store's own theater group stages live plays in its 86-seat nonprofit theater, plus there is an art gallery that didn't make the name. The 44-seat cinema specializes in foreign and lesser-known films and the Anchorage Storytellers Guild conducts readings in the summer months.

———————— • ————————

And, joining the menagerie: Minneapolis-based independent bookseller **Wild Rumpus** entices youngsters to keep coming back to buy its children's books with its own petting zoo.

———————— • ————————

The second revolution in deep-discount book selling is driven by another high-profile company whose business strategy is all about bundling. Online giant **Amazon.com** started with books, but quickly added a music store, then a video store, and then a card shop. The latest is their online auction house. And, who knows what's next in the company's fast-track march to its first billion-dollar year.

———————— • ————————

Banks offer credit cards, so . . . **Discover Card,** through its issuer, Greenwood Trust Company, offers its cardholders banking. The Discover Savers' Account, which can be accessed via ATMs and free checks, pays competitive interest at tiered rates. And, for a slightly higher return, Discover Card Certificates of Deposit lock in higher rates for terms of three months to 10 years.

Discover is also using bundling to drive use of its "ShopCenter" Web site. Nationally known retailers such as Eddie Bauer, Camelot Music, and Hickory Farms join service providers such as Discover Brokerage Direct and CBS Sports-Line to offer online merchandise and services that change year-round and offer special discounts and incentives. And, ShopCenter only takes the Discover Card.

> **Cutting prices is usually insanity if the competition can go as low as you can.**
>
> —MICHAEL PORTER,
> HARVARD BUSINESS SCHOOL

You might think that building the world's largest pet supply chain would be enough to keep customers coming back, but **PETsMART** emphasized the second half of its name by building its bundle with the founding of Vet-Smart Pet Hospital. Now, customers of the $1.7 billion Phoenix, Arizona–based chain of superstores can get veterinary services at the same place they shop for any of 12,000 pet products.

It seems like every gas station has a convenience store attached to it these days, but most of them pale before the upscale bundle Virginia-based **East Coast Oil** created to keep customers coming back to its 40 stores. In addition to low gas prices, bright lighting, clean restrooms, and employee dress codes, customers can buy an espresso, T-shirts, greeting cards, and brand-name fast food from Subway, Dunkin' Donuts, TCBY, and others.

For something a little more satisfying than fast food, check out the San Ramon, California–based **Chevron** that expanded into the growing need for take-out dining by attaching a Foodini market to its gas station. Gas up and grab the family a freshly prepared all-American meal, such as turkey and all the fixin's.

Look to the Far East for this interesting bundle: a gas station chain that sells designer apparel and accessories. Japan's **Oura Oil** communicates regularly with customers through its frequent buyer program, the Five-Up Club. When Five-Up surveys indicated that Oura's customers were also big buyers of designer consumer goods, the company started a mail-

The author once asked a man pumping gas at a filling station why his station was always so busy while the one across the street selling comparable gas at an identical price was almost always empty. This sage businessman replied, "They're in a different business than us. They're a fillin' station—we're a service station."

—Norman Augustine,
FORMER CHAIRMAN OF
MARTIN MARIETTA IN
Augustine's Laws

order operation to fill that yen—and linked it directly to the Five-Up point program to build revenue for both businesses.

————— • —————

The strategy of bundling is turning the inconvenience of going to the bank on your lunch hour into a lunch stop in its own right. Stop in at select California **Wells Fargo** branches and you can get yourself a Starbucks coffee and snacks from Briazz while you do your banking. Might as well drop off your dry cleaning at Pressing Business, too. Each operation has its own counter within the bank.

————— • —————

Banco Bradesco, Brazil's largest bank, created its own shopping mall online, partnered with major retailers to feature their wares, and named it BradescoNet. BradescoNet eliminates security concerns by simply transferring the amount of the transaction from the customer's Banco Bradesco bank account to the retail partner's Banco Bradesco bank account. Customers can also use the network to pay taxes and motor vehicle fees to governmental agencies.

————— • —————

As we've mentioned, partnering is an excellent way to create value bundles. **The Quality Services Network** is a residential services bundle that includes Merry Maids, Terminex, Tru-Green-ChemLawn, ServiceMaster, Brinks Home Security, Furniture Medic, and AmeriSpec. Merry Maids gave their customers a free "We Serve" membership (a $39.95 value) that includes a quarterly newsletter and special discounts on the services provided by member companies.

Looking for a good bundling partner? Think customer synergy. Some examples of good matches: hair salons and clothing stores; household services and lawn care; restaurants and entertainment providers; and sporting goods retailers and ticket services.

———— ● ————

Cable TV's **Discovery Channel** teamed up with Rosenbluth International to offer its armchair explorers some real-life adventures. So far, Discovery viewers can sign up for any of 14 trips, including journeys to Alaska, the Galapagos Islands, China, and Egypt.

———— ● ————

The Smithsonian Institution is a national treasure and a must-see stop on any visit to Washington, D.C., but the vast majority of the Smithsonian's visitors live too far away to be regular customers. Or do they?

Enter a bundle of benefits so juicy that it entices even those with no concrete plans to visit the museum. The Smithsonian's National Associate Membership costs $24 annually. In return, members get an annual subscription to *Smithsonian* magazine (which is worth the entire cost itself) and discounts on purchases from catalogs and gift shops.

Can't get to the nation's capital? The membership offers exclusive access to travel tours and programs around the world, and free admission to the Cooper-Hewitt Museum in New York City. And, to encourage a visit, there is also the specially priced Smithsonian Anytime Weekend in Washington that includes two night's lodging, meal coupons, an IMAX film, a behind-the-scenes tour of the Smithsonian "Castle," and two guidebooks.

———— ● ————

No need to be a world-renowned cultural institution to build a better bundle. The **Contemporary Art Center of Virginia** (CAC) attracts support and visits with a $20 annual membership that includes (among other things) free admission to all the year's shows, its newsletter, unique members-only receptions, and discounted tuition to art classes. Even better, the membership in the nonprofit is tax deductible.

———— • ————

Set up a hotel-style concierge in a real estate office and you may never have to worry about homebuyers and sellers staying loyal again. At **Coldwell Banker Jon Douglas Company,** in Mission Viejo, California, the concierge offers referrals to over 150 home-related services ranging from locksmiths to the Asian art of *feng shui* to the office's customers. The service is free to the customer, and many of the recommended vendors give discounted rates under the program.

———— • ————

Columbus, Ohio–based **H.E.R. Realtors** offers a similar service known as HOMElink. With one phone call, HOMElink connects H.E.R. customers to a range of services and utilities they are sure to need as they turn house into home. Internet service, cable, gas, electric, alarm systems, newspaper delivery, and recycling are all represented. After homebuyers are settled in, HOMElink keeps working for them with discounted services from area vendors and contractors. Again, the assistance is free to the customer.

———— • ————

Here's a neat newspaper bundle: The **Richmond-Times Dispatch** packages offers of goods and services from its advertisers and brings them to its subscribers through its Press Pass Membership Club. Subscribers can show their free membership card at over 400 local merchants to receive exclusive discounts, free samples, and special services.

———— • ————

A highly successful real estate broker once told me, "Kill your customers with service. Service, service, service. Give them so much service they'll feel guilty even thinking about doing business with someone else."

—C. BRITT BEEMER IN *PREDATORY MARKETING*

The **Automobile Association of America** is such a master of bundling that it recently has begun emphasizing its well-known initials, **AAA,** so that customers will think of it for more than its original claim to fame, emergency roadside repair service. AAA of Tidewater, Virginia, our regional branch, is typical in its large bundle of international, domestic, and local services.

There are all the logical extensions that travelers value, such as free, customized maps dubbed *TripTiks*, free guidebooks, and free American Express Traveler's Checks. Then, AAA adds in all those destination goodies. Around here you get discounts on local historical sites, tours, and museums; member rates at the Anheuser-Busch amusement parks; and a discount on oil changes at the local branch of Jiffy Lube.

AAA takes a still broader approach to bundling by addressing its members' needs at home. Now, the bundle includes discounts on such diverse items as formal wear, telephone service, and home inspections. And much more, including auto, student, and home loans, and preferred rates on financial investments such as CD's and money market funds.

————————•————————

Sprint Corporation has added roadside assistance to its cell phone bundle. Enroll in the Sprint PCS Roadside Rescue, and for $2.99 per month, you get immediate assistance either by calling a toll-free number or by dialing #ROAD on your Sprint cell phone.

————————•————————

Credit card companies are pros at bundling. In fact, the bundles they create are often developed into new products altogether, such as **American Express'** Gold Corporate Card for

Small Business. Pony up $55 annually for the card, and you get a basket of benefits including discounts on Mobil gasoline, Kinko's copy services, and FedEx shipping. Small business travelers get discounts on Hertz car rentals (and a free membership in Hertz #1 Club Gold) and at Hilton Hotels. Add in $100,000 in automatic travel insurance and free extended warranties on goods purchased with the card, and AmEx has a pretty compelling bundle.

American Express doesn't forget the merchants who accept their cards and provide the lion's share of their revenue. The $18 billion company recently offered our company, along with all the other AmEx merchants, a 20% annual rebate on long-distance telephone service from MCI.

The credit card giant doesn't stop there, either. The American Express Connections program bundles up the telephone business with a calling card featuring all the basics plus voice mail, conference calling, speed dialing, and news services. In addition to the competitive long-distance rates, the program offers members six Rewards points for every dollar spent, and your telephone bill is added to your monthly statement to cut bill paying.

Now throw in college, too. A recent American Express newsletter offered an educational loan program known as PLUS, a Federal Parent Loan for Undergraduate Students. The total cost of the education less any financial aid may be borrowed at interest rates that may not exceed 9%.

————•————

Bundles don't have to last forever. **MasterCard International** offered customers a good reason to grab their cards during the 1998 holiday season with its Holiday Savings Card

> **Find businesses who are already serving your market and create an alliance with them.**
>
> —JOE VITALE IN
> *THERE'S A CUSTOMER BORN*
> *EVERY MINUTE*

promotion. The program included discounts at over a dozen popular retailers including Gateway 2000, JCPenney, Sam Goody, The Nature Company, KB Toys, and just in case you work up an appetite from all that shopping, a price break at Pizza Hut. All you had to do to earn the discounts was use your MasterCard for the purchase.

———— ● ————

Wal-Mart Stores' **Sam's Club** is another master of bundling that takes a broad definition of its customers' needs. The fee-based wholesale club keeps customers coming back by continually adding new, discounted services to the membership bundle. For instance, Sam's Club teamed up with TTI National Long Distance to offer domestic phone rates of 9.5¢ per minute for a fee of $1 per month. Members get 100 free minutes just for signing up. Time to get online? Sam's and EarthLink Network offer members unlimited Internet access for $17.95 per month and waives the normal setup fee. Traveling on business or vacation? Call Sam's Club Travel Services for discounts of up to 30% at Ramada hotels and discounted rates at National Car Rental.

Sam's bundle keeps going: It's Club Auto program will hook you up with a participating auto dealership willing to give you a no-haggle, discounted price on the new or used car of your choice. And, its Impact Preferred Card for business customers offers supplemental healthcare coverage for everything from prescription drugs to physical therapy.

———— ● ————

Issaquah, Washington–based **Costco Companies, Inc.** jumped into residential real estate for its Costco and Price Club wholesale chain members. Costco built a network of realtors

There is only one boss: the customer. And he can fire everybody in the company, from the chairman on down, simply by spending his money somewhere else.

—SAM WALTON

and lenders willing to give commission rebates in exchange for Costco–Price Club customer referrals. Club members receive cash bonuses for using realtors and lenders referred by Costco–Price Club.

———— • ————

New Yorker magazine gives its advertisers and readers a good bundle with its "On The Town" section. A special advertising space, On the Town offers a selection of discounts and promotions designed specifically for the publication's readers. A recent issue included a discount coupon for a Broadway musical, an American Express travel package to Los Angeles, and a contest sponsored by the Jack Daniel's Distillery.

———— • ————

Martha Stewart Living Omnimedia LLC merits at least a tiara as "The Queen of Bundling." Anyone serious about the domestic arts need only take a look at the Omnimedia Guide in *Martha Stewart Living* magazine. There are the radio programs, television shows, a Web site, and personal appearances where Martha holds court. Need the products to create the lifestyle? There are the Martha-by-Mail catalogs, books, and all the tools, including that just-right bunny-shaped cookie cutter needed to make those Easter cookies in the magazine.

———— • ————

On first thought it sounds crazy to suggest bundling your products with those of your competitors, but the crazy ones may end up being those companies that reject the idea out of hand. Take a lesson from **U.S. Airways Group,** which recently started allowing its frequent flyer program members to swap its miles with **American Airlines** AAdvantage program,

Five Questions to Make Bundling Work for You

1. What services are closely associated with your products (or products with your services)?

2. When customers use your products and services, what process do they follow? How can you make it more efficient/effective?

3. What unrelated products and services do most of your customers buy and use?

4. What annual events do most of your customers observe? Can you create a special occasion bundle for each?

5. What services and products does the competition offer? How can you partner with them to bring the same to your customers?

In the global economy, a well-developed ability to create and sustain fruitful collaborations gives companies a significant competitive leg up.

—ROSABETH MOSS KANTER IN
HARVARD BUSINESS REVIEW

and vice versa. Combining miles gives customers faster rewards that are good to more destinations, allows customers to combine flights on both airlines and still earn miles, and builds business for both companies.

2

USE INCENTIVES TO DRIVE SALES

Human beings are an extraordinarily diverse lot, but we've never met anyone, rich or poor, who didn't like to get a special deal. That's why as long as people have been selling goods and services, there have been sales.

Sales are just one kind of incentive that encourages customers to do more business with you. There is, in fact, a wide array of incentives that bring customers back and even more twists and combinations on those. This chapter looks at six distinct categories of incentives. They include:

1. free gifts
2. added-value bonuses
3. coupons and rebates
4. sales
5. special financing
6. sweepstakes and contests

Incentives need not be expensive. In all the contests and sweepstakes we examined, one of our favorites involved a stuffed animal worth only

$6.99 at retail. In fact, you may already be giving your customers certain value-added extras that they don't value properly—a little publicity could go a long way in these cases.

Like every other technique for building repeat business, incentives only work when the customers find them valuable. Be sure to create yours from the customers' perspective.

There is a dark side to incentives that we should mention. They can be overused and cause customers to refuse to pay the regular selling price for your goods and services. How often have you put off a purchase, waiting for that sale that you knew would be running sometime in the near future?

When misused, incentives can also have a negative impact on profits. Witness the price wars in the airline industry in the 1980s. Special sale fares by one carrier were often matched and even bettered within the day by competing airlines. The resulting airfares were so cheap that the entire industry bled red ink.

That said, let's browse through the world of incentives.

GIVE A GIFT

They're baaack! In 1998, **McDonald's Corporation** had customers lined up for its Happy Meals, particularly when they included oh-so-popular Teenie Beanies from Ty, the maker of Beanie Babies. The freebies became instant collectibles, driving Happy Meal sales off the drive-through lane. The promotion was so successful, the company came back with a new set in 1999.

———●———

Here's another well-targeted bonus: **Trak Auto** stores recently gave customers who purchased select products and one full-price ticket a free general admission to a spectacular evening of car racing—the Friday Night of Fire. Black tie optional.

———— ● ————

Cosmetics companies have been playing the gift game for decades and few are better at it than **The Estee Lauder Companies, Inc.,** which accounts for roughly 45% of women's cosmetics sales in U.S. stores. Free gifts with purchase are a standard strategy in the company's Clinique hypoallergenic cosmetics line.

For example, Hecht's Department Store recently offered a Clinique Double Bonus promotion. With a purchase of $16.50 or more, customers received a bag including lipsticks, cleansers, moisturizer, powder, and a brush; with a purchase of $35 or more, customers also received a tote bag and portable mirror. Not only do customers go home with more than they paid for; Clinique gets to introduce them to a wide range of new products at the same time.

———— ● ————

New York City's chic make-up boutique **Shu Uemura** installed sinks throughout the store to help sell its salt scrubs and facial cleansers. Customers are invited to wash their faces, trying out as many products as they like. Afterward, they can put on a new face for free, using the store's cosmetics.

———— ● ————

Sometimes, the smallest gift is all it takes to show your customers that you appreciate them. **Merry Maids,** one of the nation's leading home and office cleaning franchises, knows that its customers have a nose for clean and so, spray an aromatic room freshener during their visits. Customers get a complimentary spray

Good customer service is no longer enough. It has to be superior, WOW, unexpected service. In a nutshell, it means doing what you say you will, when you say you will, how you say you will, at the price you promised—plus a little extra tossed in to say "I appreciate your business."

—DIANNA BOOHER,
AUTHOR AND CONSULTANT

bottle of the freshener and free refills for when that newly cleaned scent fades.

———————•———————

Campbell Soup Company made its computer-literate clientele an offer they can't refuse. Send in 10 labels from selected company products and $1.50 shipping for four free software programs. With a total retail value of over $100, each program targeted a different age group from age four to adult, so that the entire family got a gift.

———————•———————

London-based **Grand Metropolitan PLC's** Häagen-Dazs ice-cream brand keeps it customers spooning with its recent Passport to Indulgence promotion. Send in four pint-size UPC codes or the "Passports" on specially marked containers, and the company will send you a certificate for a free pint. As a bonus, you also get an entry in a $30,000 design-your-own-vacation contest.

———————•———————

Hong Kong–based **Tommy Hilfiger Corporation** earns close to $850 million a year selling the popular designer's men's clothes and licensing his name. During April 1999, the company gave away men's haircuts and styling in the department stores that carry the company's personal products. The "Clip Scenes" promotion, which kept the customers entertained with movie clips and popcorn, helped generate attention for Hilfiger's new line of men's hair-care products.

———————•———————

Erno Laszlo LLC uses a similar strategy in the high-end cosmetics market in which its products compete. Company representatives visit the department stores selling its products and pamper clients with complimentary facials, masks, and hand massages, followed by personalized makeovers with the brand-name cosmetics. It's all free to clients, and there is no obligation to make a purchase.

Always do more than is required of you.

—GEORGE S. PATTON

Attracting customers to a mall is no great feat during the holiday season, but January is a whole different story. Hampton, Virginia's **Coliseum Mall** builds business in both critical seasons with its "Mall Gift Certificates." On four specific shopping days in December, shoppers at the mall earned a free $10 gift certificate for every $150 they spent. Not so unusual, except for the fact that the gift certificates must be redeemed in the first 15 days of January, a notoriously slow shopping month.

Inner city malls have two common disadvantages: Customers disappear into the suburbs on the weekends and parking is expensive. Cleveland, Ohio's **The Avenue at Tower City Center** takes its shot at solving the problem by mailing customers "Free Weekend Parking Passes" each year. Once in the mall, customers can enjoy special events such as live performances by the famous Cleveland/San Jose Ballet or a visit with Santa, along with free gift wrapping for any purchase made at the mall.

During the 1998 holiday season, discount music chain **Music for a Song** attracted free-spending shoppers to its mall locations by offering a free CD of holiday music to its customers. In the chain's Prime Outlets location, shoppers who went to the store with $200 in same-day receipts from any of the other 85 stores in the mall received the gift.

Customers got an incentive to restrict their spending to the mall and Music for a Song got a chance to entice them with the rest of the store's merchandise.

———— • ————

Here's a smart offer from **Perdue Farms, Inc.:** Send back the company's advertised mail-in certificate with a grocery receipt that includes its chicken, and the company will send you its free Perdue Passport booklet. Inside, coupons and special orders and best of all, a collection of recipes from around the world—all of which require . . . that's right.

———— • ————

Christopher's Tavern, located in a Williamsburg hotel, has no problem generating capacity crowds during tourist season. But, it keeps residents coming back during the off-season and on a slow night, with complimentary peel and eat shrimp on Tuesdays from 5:30 to 6:30 P.M.

———— • ————

The **Whitehall Restaurant** accomplishes the same objective by adding entertainment to the menu. One night a week, the eatery brings in a band and offers dancing for diners who are light on their feet.

———— • ————

And, don't forget pizza, pizza! Detroit-based **Little Caesar Enterprises, Inc.** built the country's third largest pizza chain around its two pies for the price of one proposition. It even upped the ante to celebrate its 40th Anniversary: Buy one, get one free *and* get coupons for a free pizza and free dessert on the next visit.

———— • ————

Dallas-based superstore chain **CompUSA** makes sure software training customers keep coming back, even in the face of pending software changes with 2-for-1 offers. A recent offer covered the upcoming release of a new version of MS Office by promising a second class free when the software hit store shelves.

———— ❖ ————

Omaha Steaks often jogs repeat business for their gourmet frozen foods with extra gifts tacked on to the order. Sometimes, it's a package of hamburgers; sometimes, a New York-style cheesecake. Recently, the company advertised a free pair of "Sparkling Star Crystal Candleholders" by Mikasa as a gift incentive with the purchase of steaks.

———— ❖ ————

Gifts are also a good way to encourage former customers to come home. Washington D.C.–based **MCI Communications** woos long distance defectors with a personalized letter that begins, "We value you as a customer and we want you back." That powerful opener is followed up by an invitation to enroll in the American Airlines AAdvantage program, earning five frequent flyer miles for every dollar spent with MCI. Join back up and get a 4,000-mile bonus (paid 2,000 immediately and 2,000 after six months).

———— ❖ ————

Credit card companies are devoted gift givers, and they often tie those gifts to repeated uses of their cards. Cleveland, Ohio–based **National City Corporation** said "thank you" to its credit card holders for using their cards during the first quarter of 1999 by giving an Air Check to everyone who charged $100 on the card. The check was good for up to a $100 discount on tickets from most major airlines.

National City also gave the gift of free phone time over the 1998 holiday season.

No customer ever goes to a store merely to please the storekeeper.

—KAZUO INAMORI, FOUNDER OF KYOCERA CORPORATION

There is no such thing as a free lunch.

—**Milton Friedman,** Economist

Those who used their credit card at least three times received a free 15-minute phone card; those who charged using the card at least six times received a free 30-minute phone card. Customers did not need to do any tracking themselves; the company automatically mailed the gift in February 1999.

————— ● —————

Discover ran a similar gift promotion in September 1998. It offered a complimentary *Rand McNally Road Atlas* to those who used their card three times during the month. In October, six purchases earned a magazine subscription. In November, nine purchases earned "Box Office Bucks," two complimentary movie admissions good at any of over 1,000 participating cinemas. It wasn't quite as simple as the previous example, however; customers had to mail in a Redemption Certificate and copies of the dated receipts.

————— ● —————

Who says there's no free lunch? During a recent promotion, customers spending $55 or more at **Ukrop's Super Market** got a free meal. The $5 coupon got customers a burger, a Rueben, a stir-fry, a salad, or any of a number of other choices at the Ukrop's Grill located inside the supermarket. A smart gift that makes sure grocery shoppers get a taste of the store's extensive prepared food selection.

————— ● —————

Freebies are a good way to introduce customers to new products. Miami-based **Burger King International** received national media attention by giving away orders of its new French fries. The "Free FryDay" promotion ran at each of BK's 7,600 North American restaurants, and they gave away an estimated 15 million orders. Would you like a burger with those fries?

————— ● —————

The nation's #2 electronics superstore chain **Circuit City** teamed up with Motorola and American Express for this recent freebie. Customers who bought a Motorola pager at the chain found it came with an American Express Gift Cheque for $25. The gift check was claimed by mail and could be used anywhere the customer wished.

———————●———————

Virginia-based **Pomoco Auto Group** cross-markets its automotive repair and servicing business and thanks the buyers of new and used cars with its "Peace of Mind" Value Package. Included are four certificates good toward a free loaner car when their vehicles are in the shop.

Pomoco offers a second bonus with its unusual offer of an answering service for vacationing customers. Customers can use the dealer's toll-free telephone system to set up a phone mailbox and leave and receive messages while out of town.

———————●———————

Hall Auto World competes for car buyers with a value-added bundle it calls the Value Guarantee. Worth up to $1,920, the program includes a 7-day/1,000-mile exchange privilege, free lifetime state inspection, oil changes, towing services, discounts on routine maintenance and parts, and a free loaner car if repairs aren't done properly the first time.

———————●———————

And, here's a simple, but well-chosen gift from *Piano Today* magazine. Realizing that pianists surely know other keyboard lovers, the publication encourages them to give subscriptions as gifts with a free book of piano music entitled "Great Piano Encores."

GIVE ADDED VALUE AS A BONUS

Many purchases have "hidden" fees, those necessary extras, such as shipping, that make great added-value bonuses. **College & University Computers** offered a "dollars-and-sense" bonus in a series of ads that listed all the extras—among them, free shipping, set-up, and an extended four-year warranty—that it gives its customers. The ads tallied the free services against the actual charges for the same extras from its larger, national competitors and publicized the savings, which ran as high as $350.

In the retail book business, authors are a common added-value bonus. Like others, **Books-A-Million, Inc.** regularly hosts author readings and book signings for customers. The customers get to meet their favorite authors, autographed books are often valuable on the collector's market, and the chain keeps customers coming in.

Speaking of books: When the mass customization marketing gurus from **The Peppers and Rogers Group** released *The One to One Fieldbook*, they inserted a unique serial number in each copy. The number served as a password on the company's Web site and unlocked an added-value bonus of additional content, including "electronic tools, spreadsheets, [and] discounts."

How about a free computer with that Internet service? New York–based **Simple Solution LLC** is offering customers "The Whole Enchilada." For $19.99 per month for 48 months, you get unlimited Internet access *and* the computer you need to surf it. The deal includes free

A 1997 survey for the Incentive Federation found that U.S. businesses spend $4.23 billion annually on customer promotions.

installation in your home and a trade-in option on the computer after two years.

———— • ————

Free installation is a powerful draw for complicated and heavy products. **Bernina** sewing machines offer the state-of-the-art in the consumer market with a price to match. They sport a myriad of attachments for specialty stitching and a touch-sensitive computer screen where the thread used to be. As part of the purchase, trained technicians deliver your new machine, help set it up and situate it most advantageously, and offer a brief introduction.

———— • ————

New Jersey–based **The Hertz Corporation** eliminated one of those pesky costs that plague customers in this value-added bonus created specially for AAA members. Members who flashed their cards and a promotional coupon received a free tank of gas with their rental.

———— • ————

The Washington Post gives some extra bang for the buck to buyers of its classified car ads. It posts them at no additional charge online at washingtonpost.com's cars.com site. Buyers can use a search engine to narrow choices and sellers get greater exposure.

———— • ————

Here's a simple bonus that customers appreciate: **Sunglass Hut International** says, "stop by anytime for a free tune-up" when it sells a pair of shades. The staff will happily clean and adjust your glasses without charge as long as you own them. They will also be happy to show you the newest technology and latest styles, as long as you're there.

———— • ————

Leading book wholesaler **Ingram Book Company** encourages larger single orders by offering

> Render more service for that which you are paid and you will soon be paid for more than you render.
>
> —NAPOLEON HILL

free shipping on telephone orders of 100 books or more over the telephone. Order electronically, a practice that cuts the company's costs, and free shipping kicks in at 50 titles.

———— ● ————

Competitor **Baker & Taylor, Inc.** set its free shipping offer at a lower level. Telephone orders of 50 books from your assigned Baker & Taylor warehouse receive free freight regardless of whether the books are available or not. Order 100 books from any two warehouses and get free freight from both.

———— ● ————

Take a step back up the supply chain and you'll find publishing giant **Simon & Schuster, Inc.** offering free freight on its trade book orders from booksellers. Anyone who has ever hefted a carton of books knows that free shipping is a powerful incentive for repeat business.

———— ● ————

Even high-style women's attire retailer **Cache, Inc.** jumped on the free shipping bandwagon. The New York City–based store chain and American Express teamed up to build catalog sales and card use with the incentive. Customers using the American Express card for catalog purchases automatically received free shipping on their order.

———— ● ————

And, finally, place your order for well-known clothing brands such as L'eggs, Champion, and Hanes on cataloger **One Hanes Place's** Web site, enter the special code on your catalog, and you get free shipping. Both company and customer save money on the orders, which do not require a customer service operator.

———— ● ————

We thought it was excessive when even shipping companies started adding shipping fees to

Good products, bad products. Businesses survive with both. But there's one thing no business has enough of: customers.

—HARVEY MACKAY IN
BEWARE THE NAKED MAN WHO
OFFERS YOU HIS SHIRT

their shipping rates, but then overnight package shipper **FedEx** waived its $3-per-package pickup fee to build volume among small business members in the FedEx Spotlight Program. "Eliminating the $3 package pickup charge is another way for us to show how much we value your business," says the company's personalized letter.

The invitation to join the free program also included a coupon for $20 off a FedEx package shipment and a calendar filled with small business success stories, FedEx news, and tips on free services and special benefits.

———— • ————

Tandy Corporation's RadioShack chain encourages customers to use its in-store Answer-Plus credit card with a basket of value-added bonuses. AnswerPlus customers get special discounts, express checkout, no payment/no interest for up to 90 days at the customer's request, 10% off batteries, free gift boxes, and priority repair service.

———— • ————

The customer who is willing to pay list price for products and services is a valuable commodity, and **Northwest Airlines** knows it. So, it makes sure the full-fare traveler has a good reason to fly with them. Customers who buy a full-fare Coach ticket on qualifying flights get an automatic upgrade to First Class at no additional charge, along with 1,000 extra miles in their WorldPerks frequent flyer account.

Northwest teamed up with VISA to target business flyers with this bonus: Frequent Flyer club WorldPerks' members using the VISA card to purchase a First or World Business Class ticket to Asia received a free roundtrip domestic ticket on the airline.

Mix It Up

It's helpful to categorize incentives into two broad types: hard and soft.

- **Hard incentives** are benefits that customers would normally pay for and therefore, cost you hard dollars. They include a sale or a cash rebate.

- **Soft incentives** are value-added extras that the customer may value highly, but whose cost may be negligible to you. For example, customers value both a ride home from the auto dealership where their car is being serviced or a free upgrade to an otherwise empty seat on a jet.

So, it pays to create a mix of both benefit types when designing incentive programs.

Every company's greatest assets are its customers, because without customers there is no company.

—MICHAEL LEBOEUF,
AUTHOR OF *THE GREATEST MANAGEMENT PRINCIPLE IN THE WORLD*

—————— ● ——————

Celebrity Cruises took the free upgrade idea out to sea when it teamed up with American Express to create its own free upgrade incentive. Customers who used the American Express card to buy an Alaskan cruise vacation on the Celebrity ship *Mercury* received a free upgrade to the next level of rooms.

—————— ● ——————

For those who prefer to ride the rails, **Amtrak** ran this special designed to attract families. Buy one full-price ticket, get the second one for half price, and the third free.

—————— ● ——————

Knowing that there are plenty of two–cell-phone families out there, Little Rock, Arkansas–based telecommunication company **Alltel Corporation** put second numbers on sale for its existing customers. Alltel offered six months of free access on each 18-month contract.

—————— ● ——————

Long-distance phone service provider **Sprint** rewards small business customers who sign up with them with free domestic long-distance calls every Friday for up to 110 consecutive weeks. As long as customers commit to spending at least $50 per month, they qualify for up to $1,000 worth of free Friday calls per month.

SATISFY COUPON-CUTTERS AND REBATE-COLLECTORS

Coupons are a time-honored tradition in the grocery business and quickly add up to substantial savings for those shoppers who can muster the discipline needed to collect and redeem them. The Jacksonville, Florida, supermarket chain **Winn-Dixie Stores, Inc.** is one of many in the industry that keeps customers coming back by periodically doubling and tripling the face value of coupons. In one recent promotion, coupons up to 50¢ were tripled up to the full purchase price of the item on sale. Winn-Dixie doesn't rely completely on its vendors for incentives. It also builds business with its own coupons. A recent mailing offered four $5 savings certificates applicable to purchases over $25.

———————⬤———————

Casual eatery **Shackleford's** introduced its newest location to our local market with money-saving newspaper coupons. Patrons had a choice of a second dinner entrée at half price or $5 off any two lunches.

———————⬤———————

Point-of-purchase coupons are a fine repeat business builder and virtually any company can use them. If you ate at a **Hard Rock Café** during September 1998, you received a $5 discount certificate valid for food and beverage purchases on your next visit.

———————⬤———————

Everybody's got his or her own credit card these days. Use the **Omaha Steaks'** Platinum Plus Visa card, and 5% of all Omaha Steak purchases and 1% of all other purchases made on the card rack up points towards $25 "Omaha Steaks Certificates" that may be used for any item sold by the company.

———————⬤———————

The Discovery Channel, one of the popular cable stations owned by Maryland-based **Discovery Communications, Inc.,** also uses coupons to promote its *Platinum Plus* MasterCard. Once approved, new cardholders receive a $20 coupon for purchases made at company's Nature Company and Discovery stores and catalogs. To keep buyers using their card, a new

An America's Research Group study found that when supermarkets began offering double coupon promotions, readership of the advertising inserts in the typical Sunday newspaper rose from around 40 to 74%.

Customer service is American Express's patent protection. Our goal, simply stated, is to be the best.

—JAMES ROBINSON, FORMER CEO OF AMERICAN EXPRESS

$20 coupon is sent each time purchases add up to $1,500. Transfer the balances from other credit cards and get another freebie—a $50 Discovery Channel fleece pullover.

———————●———————

Here's a neat twist on double coupons: From February 1, 1999, through April 30, 1999, members in the **American Express** Membership Rewards program got double points (redeemable in air miles and merchandise) for using their card at supermarkets and drug stores. Not only did the promotion encourage customers to use the American Express card; it built the company's share in specific market sectors.

———————●———————

Morgan Stanley Dean Witter Co.'s Discover Card built its business on the Cashback Bonus, a rebate check for 1% of its cardholders' annual purchases, but it doesn't stop there. For every purchase up to a maximum of $2,500 charged on the card in August and September 1998, Discover automatically credited customers' October and November billing statements an additional rebate of 1%—in effect doubling their own Cashback Bonus in order to stimulate card use.

———————●———————

Although Bentonville, Arkansas–based **Sam's Club** doesn't accept manufacturer's coupons meant for retailers, they have found a great way to drive sales with manufacturer's rebates. The wholesale club highlights manufacturers' refund offers in a monthly flier including a photo, amount of refund, and exact purchase requirements. Members who buy those items simply fill out the single rebate form in the flier and mail it to Sam's Club along with their receipt. The company does the rest, sending rebate checks to members within two months.

Bank of America unveiled a new service exclusively for its Advantage-level customers, dubbed Advantage Values. Advantage Values are discount and rebate offers made to clients by nationally known companies—from which the bank receives no compensation.

One of those offers from the **Holland America** cruise line offered Advantage Values Travel Credits for Alaskan cruises. Members earn credits in the amount of 3 to 5% of the price of trip, which can then be applied toward a second cruise within 24 months.

Teaming up to distribute coupons is a good idea. Recently, outlet mall shoppers at **Liz Claiborne** received point of sale coupons for a 15% discount at the **Mikasa Factory Store** just across the way.

RUN A SALE

Who deserves sale prices more than your existing customers? Within weeks of sending you a shipment of their premium meats, seafood, and other specialty food items, Nebraska's **Omaha Steaks, Inc.** starts an incentive blitz. The company figures out how long it should take you to finish off your order, and then offers specials and discounts ranging up to $30 off the regular price to earn a re-order.

Retailers are pros at using sales as incentives to bring customers back into their stores. **Hecht's** department stores recently ran a "lowest prices of the season" spring sale on selected, popular merchandise and raised sales in a slow part of the day with "early bird" specials in the morning hours of the first day of the event.

————— ◉ —————

German media giant Bertelsmann's **BMG Music Service** keeps its members buying with regular sales. Deals such as "Buy 1, Get 3 FREE" and "Get Unlimited Selections at 70% Off" are common; and even when no special promotion is in progress, any CD purchased at regular price enables customers to receive a 50% discount on all other CDs purchased at the same time.

————— ◉ —————

Sneaker emporium **Just For Feet** created a sure-fire way to keep customers coming back. It ran a "Spend a Dollar, Get a Dollar" sale, where any amount spent in the store generated a gift certificate for that exact amount. The catch: the gift certificates could not be used until several months later, generating two visits out of one for the chain.

Here's another idea from the sneaker king: Just For Feet was giving trade-ins to customers bringing in their old, worn-out athletic shoes during a recent promotion. It discounted a new pair by $5 to 15 depending on their cost.

————— ◉ —————

Even an education can be put on sale: Virginia is one of several states offering sale prices to resident parents willing to pay in advance for their children's education. The **Virginia Prepaid Education Program** uses an advance lump sum payment or installment plan to guarantee tuition costs as low as 30% of today's rates. Parents get peace of mind and a great price; the state's educational institutions get the customers they will need in the future.

————— ◉ —————

Want an educational savings vehicle with more flexibility? Try the **Virginia Education**

Savings Trust, a new trust offering tax-deferred growth on up to $100,000 in contributions. This one is good for in-state or out-of-state students and can be used for room, board, books, and other college expenses beyond tuition.

———— ⚫ ————

Sales are a good answer to those natural lulls in the business calendar, such as weekends at airport hotels. The **Wyndham Garden Hotel** works to fill its empty rooms at the Richmond Airport using $64 room rates on Friday, Saturday, and Sunday. Guests also wake up to a complimentary full breakfast and a leisurely, late 3:00 P.M. checkout on Sunday.

———— ⚫ ————

The Ritz-Carlton Hotel Company put special weekends, such as a Spring Getaway, Memorial Day, and Labor Day, on sale exclusively to American Express cardholders. It includes rates as low as $88 per night at any one of 24 Ritz-Carlton City Hotels and Resorts. Not bad for a first-class hotel in some of the world's most desirable locations.

———— ⚫ ————

The **Holiday Inn** recently ran its Weekender packages at special rates. Why stay with this chain? They included a free entry in the *Good Morning America* Stay, Play and Win contest, which paid off in an expense-paid trip to New York City and lots of other prizes.

———— ⚫ ————

The **Rail Europe Group** celebrated the 40th anniversary of the establishment of its popular Eurailpass with this creative sale: it offered everyone else who turned 40 along with the pass in 1999 a 40% discount off of its regular price. Oh, and if you're not exactly 40, it promises discounts for you, too.

———— ⚫ ————

The 12-store **Video Update** chain slows down on weeknights, so it created sales on those nights. On Monday, Wednesday, and Thursday, customers can rent three movies for the price of two. On Tuesday, every movie is only 99¢.

————— ❖ —————

Today's best deals in air travel are online. Atlanta-based **Delta Air Lines, Inc.** fills its underbooked weekend flights with short-notice deep discounts available only through its Web site. The carrier posts its specials on Wednesday, and the flights depart that Saturday, returning the following Monday or Tuesday.

————— ❖ —————

American Airlines has a similar program offering daily "NetSAAver Fares." Sign up at the company's Web site and American will e-mail you the sale fares daily. A recent roundtrip from Washington D.C. to Miami was $149; or for holders of air miles, $39 with the redemption of 13,000 miles.

There is a further incentive to log on to American's site. To encourage customers to move online for ticketing and payment, a money-saver for the company, it offers a 1,000-air-mile bonus after each flight booked online. To get them started, American offers an additional 3,000 bonus miles for the first flight taken.

————— ❖ —————

Continental Airlines created C.O.O.L. Travel Specials, an on-request, weekly e-letter that sells its less-traveled weekend flights at deep discounts. Continental makes a full package out of each flight by partnering with hotels and rental car companies that also offer discounts good for when you reach your destination.

————— ❖ —————

The season ticket is another form of sale that keeps 'em coming back. **The Cleveland Orchestra** warms up for its formal season during the summer at Akron, Ohio's Blossom Music Center. They get listeners back for two and three performances each weekend by selling lawn tickets to the outdoor concerts in 10-ticket books for about the same price as a single cheap seat during the formal run. There's even a free upgrade deal: two of the tickets can be traded for the amphitheater's indoor seats.

Like many theme parks, Anheuser-Busch Companies, Inc.'s **Busch Gardens** keeps its rides full with season passes. For around $90, customers get unlimited free admissions, free parking, and 10% discounts on gift shop purchases and meals. After the first year, pass holders can renew over the telephone at a still-higher discount.

Oh, that crazy Chihuahua! **Taco Bell** is capitalizing on its hugely popular Chihuahua ads with a sale offer that should even satisfy the hungriest families. Dubbed "10 for 10," customers can get 10 tacos or burritos, an order of nachos, and the chain's Mexican pizza for $9.99. Need more? Add five more tacos or burritos for $3. And, that's not all folks. Taco Bell topped it off with a coupon for a free five-night Blockbuster movie rental.

Blockbuster Entertainment Corporation loves getting its coupons into customer's hands, no matter where they are. Recently, customers renting cars at Thrifty Car Rental were thanked with a Blockbuster Value Card good for one free movie rental. Eligible frequent flyer renters can choose two movie cards or frequent flyer miles.

———— • ————

Dillard's department store chain differentiates its sales in a sales-driven industry by packaging them as events. One recent example was the Cosmetics Garden Party, a weekend sale that included "festive entertainment, music, and complimentary gift wrap on all cosmetics and fragrances selected." The parties also included beverages and snacks, registries to win museum passes and fragrance baskets, free gifts with $40 purchases, and free satin gift boxes for purchases over $55.

———— • ————

Hecht's department stores countered with "Perfect Fit Week." In addition to 30% discounts on famous brands of brassieres, Perfect Fit Week features the expertise of manufacturer's representatives and Hecht's own fit specialists. Women buying new bras are interviewed, measured, and fitted for the perfect size and style.

GIVE BETTER FINANCE TERMS

"Buy now, pay later" is a much heard refrain these days for very good reason. The purchase of high-priced merchandise is more often determined by the customers' ready cash than their desire to buy. Upscale Virginia furniture store **Willis Wayside** uses a common solution to that problem with promotions involving their in-store charge card. When Willis wants to build business, it eliminates the interest, and sometimes even the payment itself, on purchases made with their card. For example, purchases made on the Willis card during April 1998 required no down payment and were interest-and payment-free for one year.

————●————

Dallas, Texas–based cataloger **Horchow Home Collection** features high-priced furniture and accessories, but they keep even budget-conscious customers coming back with their flexible payment plans. To help their customers decorate their homes and offices in high style, Horchow offers the "Extended Payment Plan" on purchases of $250 or more. Under the plan, the customer's credit card is charged in five equal monthly installments. The best part of this arrangement is that there are no interest charges on the remaining balance and no additional cost for this service.

————●————

Bloomingdale's department store chain created a special financing deal to encourage customers to make their large purchases of fine china, crystal, and silver all at once. The Dining Circle Club allows customers purchasing over $200 worth of this merchandise on their Bloomingdale's charge accounts to extend their payments over 12 months without any interest charges at all. Even better, it's a separate line of credit, so you can still charge away on your card.

————●————

Reliable Home Office offers a similar program on its big-ticket furniture and electronics products. The catalog "tags" items eligible for a 0% interest, extended-payment plan. The cost is then billed over four months to customers' credit card. Add in the 30-day money-back guarantee and free return shipping for compelling reasons to buy from Reliable.

————●————

Want to encourage business from prompt-paying customers and improve cash flow at the same time? Try the time-honored "2%10" offer. **Ingram Book Company** offers customers

> Satisfied customers are an organization's most successful salespeople, because they do not stand to benefit financially from recommending the organization to others.
>
> —Eberhard Schueing in *Creating Customers for Life*

who are willing to pay their monthly statements by the 10th of the month an additional 2% discount off their bills. Customers reduce the cost of goods sold and Ingram cuts its receivables cycle.

————— ● —————

And, don't forget discounts for advance payments. National franchiser **TruGreen-ChemLawn's** service is based on an annual seven-visit program. To lock customers in and jump-start revenues, the company offers those who prepay their annual service in a lump sum, a 10% discount on the entire package.

HAVE A CONTEST

The online world is a hotbed of contests and sweepstakes designed to keep customers coming back. In early 1998, EZVenture, a site catering to the small business Web surfer that was created by **Yoyodyne** (and now owned by **Yahoo!**), kept its customers coming back on a daily basis with ongoing contests featuring something every small business owner needs . . . working capital. Visitors to the site could enter the contest with a simple click of the mouse once per day or via mail up to 1,000 times. The grand prize: $100,000 toward any business they choose and, of course, no purchase is required.

————— ● —————

MSNBC keeps customers coming back to their news-based site with a similar strategy. Each daily visit entitles the surfer to a free entry in a contest for frequent flyer miles. Once a month, one lucky winner gets 100,000 miles; once a day, one winner gets 30,000 miles; and 10 times per day, even more winners get 5,000 miles each.

————— ● —————

Microsoft did the same with its newly opened virtual store. Visitors until May 1999 earned a chance to win a daily prize of $500 of the company's software. Be the 100,000th entry each day and you get a $1,000 shopping spree. It's a great traffic builder at very little cost to the software giant.

———— • ————

HGTV, the home and garden cable channel, grabbed some serious repeat business on its Web site with its annual "Dream House Give-away." Surfers were allowed to enter once daily via the site and the contest generated over four million separate entries. The 1999 winner got a package worth over $600,000 that included a brand-new, fully furnished Florida beach house and a luxury sports utility vehicle for four-wheeling in the sand.

———— • ————

Amazon.com drove its sales for the latest legal thriller from John Grisham with the "$25,000 Street Lawyer Contest." The best part was, even those players who didn't win got a $5 electronic gift certificate applicable to any book order made in the next 15 days. Everybody wins, including the online bookseller.

———— • ————

In 1998, **General Motors** kept its customers using the GM MasterCard all year with the "Use It—Drive It Sweepstakes." Every time you used the card for a purchase of over $25, you received an automatic entry in the contest, which gave two winners each month a new GM car or truck and 1,000 runners-up every month a free 45-minute MCI PrePaid Phone Card.

———— • ————

During the first two months of 1999, **Discover** tapped into the big celebration of the new millenium by automatically entering all its charging customers in its own sweepstakes. Grand prize: a trip to New York City for the Times Square 2000 celebration along with a $2,000 Discover Card credit.

———— • ————

Magazine publishers are contest experts. They use them to keep subscribers re-upping each year, a prerequisite for keeping their advertising rates plump and juicy. Last year, **Worth** magazine enticed readers to renew their subscriptions with an offer of 50% off the cover price. They also threw in a shot at "Instant Riches," a well-targeted sweepstakes with a prize of $75,000 and a session with "one of the country's 60 top financial advisors." The winner picked the advisor and *Worth* paid for the entire visit, including airfare.

———— • ————

One of our local florists, **Flower Shoppe of Williamsburg,** cashed in on the Beanie Babie craze by holding a drawing to win one of the enormously popular Princess Beanie Babies that were created as a memorial to the late Princess Diana. With a value of up to $350 on the collector's market, the drawing for a $6.99 stuffed animal created long lines of customers and local media attention at almost no cost to the store.

———— • ————

In 1998, Charlotte, North Carolina–based **Pepsi Cola Bottling Company** celebrated Pepsi's 100th anniversary and made a grab for a whole new generation of Pepsi drinkers at the same time. It partnered with over 130 local hospitals to give one share of company stock to the first baby born at each hospital that year. And just so none of the newborns felt left out, the company gave each baby born on New Year's Day a gift package worth about $100.

———————— • ————————

You can't win if you don't play. But, that doesn't mean that there aren't millions of losing lottery tickets. City daily newspaper **The Richmond Times-Dispatch** used those tickets to build its readership with a creative contest dubbed "Second Chance Lotto." Every Sunday, six lottery numbers are placed in ads throughout the paper and two additional winning numbers are placed in newspaper ads each weekday. If your losing tickets match the numbers, mail them in, and the paper draws a $5,000 winner and a $1,000 winner from the tickets each week.

———————— • ————————

Belgian-based **Godiva Chocolatier,** a subsidiary of Campbell Soup Company, keeps customers returning in the lucrative Valentine's Day market with an annual contest that makes a box of its gourmet chocolates even more special. Buy a specially marked box of Godiva and get a chance to win the grand prize of a 7-carat diamond ring or one of 100 first prizes, a pair of diamond earrings.

———————— • ————————

And, never forget Mother's Day! **Hallmark's** Gold Crown teamed up with United Airlines to capture a bigger share of the card and gift business for that big day with its "In Honor of Mother's Day" contest. The winner received two roundtrip tickets anywhere in the continental U.S., which we're sure they used to go see Mom.

———————— • ————————

Blue Ridge Mountain Sports, a chain of outdoor recreation stores, appealed to its adventurous clientele with a contest offering a

> **Question: What's the difference between winning a cereal bowl on Dish Night and a winning a Super Bowl ticket? Answer: There isn't any. Motivate your customers with incentives and they'll do what you want them to.**
>
> —HARVEY MACKAY IN
> *PUSHING THE ENVELOPE*

trip for two to exotic Patagonia, located in Southern Chile and Argentina. No purchase necessary; just a visit to the store.

———————•———————

Supermarkets have embraced the contest strategy in a big way. To encourage shoppers to use the **Ukrop's** Valued Customer (UVC) card and enhance the sales of certain products, the chain runs monthly sweepstakes. In February 1999, customers using their UVC card to buy specific sponsors' products were automatically entered for a free trip for two to the Division I NCAA Men's Basketball Championship in St. Petersburg, Florida. To drive Web site traffic, the grocer also offered 10 winners a $1,000 "Grocery Give-a-Way" Internet Sweepstakes for UVC cardholders who visited the site.

———————•———————

Not to be outdone, the Salisbury, North Carolina–based **Food Lion** chain encourages shoppers to use their frequent shopper card when making purchases with automatic entries in the $10 billion grocer's $1,000,000 Give-away. Customers receive one free entry for every dollar spent and 10 bonus entries for every specially designated sale item purchased, up to 200 entries per card per person. The odds may not be a whole lot better, but it's certainly cheaper than the lottery.

———————•———————

NationsBank, recently merged with Bank of America, used its 1998 "Magic Moments" contest as the basis for a major advertising campaign during the holidays. For two months, each day had one magic moment, a one-second interval when any purchase made on the NationsBank Visa card was free, no matter how much was charged.

———— ◉ ————

General Motor's Buick division recently kept potential customers coming back to its dealerships by giving away a car a day for 45 days. Customers collected game pieces from newspaper and magazine inserts, at a Buick dealer, or over the phone or Internet. Then, they brought one game piece per day to a Buick dealer to determine whether they had won a new car.

———— ◉ ————

Sneaker retailer **Just For Feet** uses basketball courts, snack bars, and sports videos to keep customers coming back. It also used the game piece gambit to promote sales of Reebok DMX series athletic shoes for one week in April 1999. Customers who try on a pair of the shoes got a game piece for their trouble. The winner of the contest got a cool million for new sneaks.

———— ◉ ————

McDonald's Corporation created a contest around a game that transcends generational gaps, Parker Bros.' Monopoly. The contest comes complete with a board and property/ prize pieces. Customers collect game pieces by purchasing select items at the leading fast-food chain. The pieces offer instant winnings for free food and cash giveaways, or they are matched to earn prizes up to $1 million.

———— ◉ ————

TRICON Global Restaurants, Inc., parent of Taco Bell, Pizza Hut, and KFC, countered with a Star Wars contest that includes all three chains. The game pieces, which feature characters from the movie, include a variety of instant prizes, and when combined in complete sets, pay off in one of three $1 million jackpots.

———— ◉ ————

> We think it's important for people to just come in and have a good time.
>
> —Harold Ruttenburg,
> CEO of Just For Feet

Sunglass Hut International, Inc. used the instant winner technique in a recent contest. When Daylight Savings time kicked in, customers received an enticing postcard in the mail: Purchase a pair of Ray-Ban, Killer Loop, or Revo shades and get a free instant game card. Winning prizes included a trip to the Cannes Film Festival to show off those new shades.

———————●———————

Best Buy Company, Inc. doesn't want its customers buying ties for Father's Day. So, it ran the Digital Dad Sweepstakes. Sign up online for a chance to win a complete digital entertainment system, which Dad can pick up at a nearby Best Buy on his day.

———————●———————

Mobil Oil and **American Airlines** covered all the bases when they offered the air carrier's frequent flyers a reason to fuel up at Mobil stations. Every tank of gas came with a three-way-to-win game packet. In it was a Match & Win game good for an instant win of up to 10,000 frequent flyer miles or one of 1,300 roundtrips on American Airlines; a Collect For Miles game giving air miles for every five game pieces collected; and, an Enter & Win game which was mailed in for a chance to win the Grand Prize of free air travel for a year on American or one of five First Prizes—one-week vacations for two.

———————●———————

And, don't forget the time-honored one-millionth customer contest. **AMC Hampton Town Centre 24** is Virginia's largest cinema, big enough to serve 1 million moviegoers a year. The theater announced the estimated month of the event and offered to reward the millionth customer with a prize package containing 24 movie passes, a shopping spree, and movie merchandise.

———————— • ————————

In a very competitive market, long distance service **10-10-345** gives callers a good reason to keep dialing in to their access number. Every call generates a chance to win a grand prize of $1 million and other prizes, including roundtrip airline tickets, electronics, and phone cards.

———————— • ————————

Tie contests to larger promotional campaigns for maximum impact. In 1997, when **Sara Lee Corporation** sponsored Tina Turner's "Wildest Dreams" North American tour, Sara Lee subsidiary Hanes also signed up the rock star as their spokesperson. The company built a series of contests for their retailer customers around Turner and the tour. Macy's, for example, invited their New York customers to showcase their own talents by singing in a contest to win free admission to a Tina Turner concert at Radio City Music Hall. It worked: that day, hosiery sales were up 42%.

———————— • ————————

How about letting customers choose their own contest prize? Furniture retailer **Willis Wayside** periodically runs its "Heart's Desire" promotion. It's a customized giveaway: Choose your favorite item in the store and register to win it. Those who cannot wait can purchase the item with an extra 5% discount and still get a full refund if their ticket comes in.

3

TAP INTO COMMUNITIES OF INTEREST

A community of interest is a group of people connected by a common thread. Political parties, religions, and nations are all communities of interest. So are less-exalted groups, such as fan clubs and Internet chat rooms.

People, and that means your customers too, look for others who share their interests. And the people who buy your services and products may well find value in sharing that experience with others who do the same.

Developing communities of interest often adds status to a product. Think about Beanie Babies. If so many people are so crazy about them, they must be valuable. Right? Communities of interest also generate customer traffic. No one goes to a Harley motorcycle rally not wanting to see Harleys.

Companies that create a connection between customers build a powerful mechanism for repeat business. A community of interest can help turn a simple transaction between buyer and seller into a relationship. At the same time, it gives customers an emotional connection to your company, a connection that may last generations.

CREATE YOUR OWN COMMUNITY

The loyalty of the owners of **Harley-Davidson** motorcycles is legendary. Just ask a Harley rider if they would buy another make of motorcycle, and be prepared for a pithy response. And, we're not talking outlaws these days; the typical Harley owner is married with children, has at least some college, and earns over $60,000 per year.

The loyalty of Harley owners generated its own community of riders, who have little trouble recognizing each other, especially those on the low-slung, heavyweight "hogs" with the distinctive roar. And, these days, neither does the company, which flirted with complacency and bankruptcy in the 1970s, and then saw the light.

Purchase a new Harley-Davidson and it comes with a free, one-year HOG (Harley Owner's Group) membership. Members are invited to any of 50 company-sponsored "HOG" events annually; they attract about 400,000 riders every year. After the first year, membership is $35 per year. And, last time we checked, member rolls had swelled to over 360,000—a huge audience for new bikes, branded clothing, toys, and even H-D deodorant!

———— ● ————

Creating a family of owners also became an early retention strategy for General Motor's subsidiary **Saturn.** Buy a Saturn, and every year, you are invited to the company-sponsored Saturn Homecoming in Spring Hill, Tennessee. Owners attend from across the nation, gathering for family fun, country western music, picnics, and factory tours.

———— ● ————

Germany's **Volkswagen Group** offers customers in its home country a free membership

If you can persuade your customer to tattoo your name on their chest, they probably will not switch brands.

—UNIDENTIFIED PROFESSOR
ON HARLEY OWNERS

in the Volkswagen Club. The Club's service center is open every day and offers directions, ticket and event reservations, a club card, magazine, and special partner incentives. Members earn points for automobile service, parts, and maintenance purchases over $50. Points, valued at $1 per 100, can be used to pay dealers for service or new cars.

Volkswagen of North America has its own VW Club. The American version includes 30 minutes free long distance on a "rechargeable phone card," an official club T-shirt, a road atlas, a travel book, a newsletter, an optional credit card, and special event invitations. There is a fee of $25 per year.

———•———

DaimlerChrysler's Jeep division created Camp Jeep, an exclusive event for Jeep owners and their guests. In 1999, the fifth annual three-day romp was held in Virginia's Blue Ridge Mountains. For $225 per Jeep (the price includes everyone in the vehicle), participants enjoy 4-wheeling, tubing, fly-fishing, and other outdoor activities befitting fun-loving, Jeep-owning adventurers.

———•———

Irish crystal-maker **Waterford,** whose distinctive designs are often flattered by imitation, started catering to the community of collectors interested in its products by establishing the Waterford Society. Customers who join the club at the $45 annual membership rate get good value for their money. On enrollment, they receive a hand-cut vase valued at $65. In addition, members receive *Waterford Reflections*, a quarterly magazine, invitations to special events, and exclusive access to private collection and limited-edition purchases.

Make a customer, not a sale.

—KATHERINE BARCHETTI,
FOUNDER K. BARCHETTI SHOPS

———— ● ————

Hungarian ceramic figurine maker **Herend Porcelain Manufactory Ltd.** has created the Herend Guild for its community of collectors. In return for the membership fee, collectors are offered a new limited edition piece each year, as well as regular news about the company's products.

———— ● ————

It sounds contrary, but sometimes community building means refusing to fulfill demand. When **Enesco Group's** Precious Moments figurines generated extraordinary demand, the founder of the company refused to ramp up production. By channeling customer demand into new figurines instead of filling the demand for each existing figurine, the company fed collector fever and drove sales in the long term.

———— ● ————

The current craze for **Ty Inc.'s** Beanie Babies is a similar situation. The company is selling hundreds of million of dollars worth of the small stuffed animals by "retiring" them. Its customers can't walk into a store and simply buy one of each, and collector fever grows.

———— ● ————

How about building a community around the packaging for your product? When Austrian Eduard Hass invented PEZ mints for smokers in 1927, he probably never envisioned PEZ-heads, collectors of the pop-up dispensers of the candy. Connecticut-based **PEZ Candy, Inc.** gets a big boost from its community of collectors. They help buy something like three billion pieces of the candy in a wide variety of dispensers, topped with such favorites as Disney and Star Wars figures, each year.

———— ● ————

Small communities can be just as strong as their bigger kin. **Pottery Wine & Cheese Shop,** a small chain of wine merchants, created a community with its Wine Tasters Society. For $30 per month, the store offers two bottles of specially chosen wine, delivered to its members before it is offered to the general public, and special pricing on additional bottles.

This is not your usual sports equipment store. There's a 65-foot climbing wall to try out the climbing equipment, a biking trail to try out the wheels, a Rain Room to test the water-proofing, and even a pool of brackish water to check out the water purifiers. **Recreational Equipment, Inc.** (REI) is a Seattle-based sporting goods cooperative founded on the idea of community by a group of mountaineers in 1938. The cooperative's 1.4 million members pay the $15 initiation fee in exchange for a 10% annual rebate on purchases and a vote at company meetings. But more importantly, it created a community that supports the company with loyalty and over a half-billion dollars in annual revenues.

You don't have to go so far as to create a co-operative to become a destination for a community. Rockville, Maryland–based **Hudson Trail Outfitters** also brought the outdoors in for their customers. The store's rain cave and climbing wall encourage customers to get hands-on with products and blur the line between shopping and entertainment.

The very nature of your product may create an instant community. Witness the software industry, which derives much of its value from the captive market for ever-more potent product

We need a good story and we are willing to pay for it.

—ROLF JENSEN IN *THE DREAM SOCIETY*

upgrades. **Intuit, Inc.** captures a lion's share of the repeat business by going directly to its customers. When the company releases a new version of its financial software, it mails customers the news, along with early response discounts and freebies.

―――――●―――――

A little personality can go a long way in community building. Fast-growing furniture and housewares retailer **Restoration Hardware** adds personality to its marketing mix in the form of personal notes. Founder and CEO Stephen Gordon writes one for each of the over 900 items the store sells. The notes are between 100 and 400 words long, and they describe the appeal of the merchandise, a history, a warm memory. The notes create a sort of community among the shoppers who relate to them. They aren't just shopping; they are learning and sharing fond memories at the same time.

―――――●―――――

Specialty retailer **Wild Birds Unlimited** is expert at focusing in on its well-defined community of customers. In addition to just the right seed or mix to attract just about any bird in the area, Wild Birds Unlimited also takes their patrons to the birds. It regularly sponsors walks, lectures, and trips designed to educate and delight its bird-watching clientele. In early 1999, our local store offered regional trips to the James River and Point of Rocks Park and a presentation on backyard bird feeding.

―――――●―――――

Newport News, Virginia–based **Hutchens Chevrolet** turns the inevitable questions owners have about their new vehicles into a community-building event. Customers of the dealership are invited to regularly held open houses known as "Getting to Know You." In addition to refreshments and door prizes, customers can talk to dealer representatives about their new cars. Questions about their new vehicles as well as advice on maintenance, safety, and warranty issues are addressed in a relaxed atmosphere; and Hutchens gets a chance to win a customer for life.

— • —

Santa Monica, California–based retailer **Big Dog Sportswear** sells specialty clothing that prominently features the chain's red-tongued dog logo. For consumers who go for this sort of thing in a big way, the company has also created the Big Dogs Club. The Big Dogs Club costs members $15 every year, and in return they receive a newsletter, decals and a handbook, exclusive product offers, advance sales notice, and discounts from partners, including Iams Pet Foods, Hawaiian Hotels, Polaroid, Sea World, and others. Give an additional $3 to Big Dog's nonprofit foundation and you're a Top Dog.

— • —

Yahoo's VP of Direct Marketing Seth Godin is a leading advocate of Permission Marketing and author of a book of the same name. In it, Godin describes five incremental steps to "dating" customers, a process we think is a lot like community building:

1. Give them an incentive for joining up—a sweepstakes entry or e-letter.
2. Over time, start to teach them about you.
3. Reinforce permission with fresh, and customized, incentives.
4. Get more permission with more valuable incentives.
5. Begin to create profit from permission.

Norwalk, Connecticut–based **Stew Leonard's Dairy Store** is legendary for its fabulous customer service. One way it bags customers is the store's quirky photo exhibit: When a Stew Leonard's shopping bag found its way into a customer's vacation photograph, the store put it on display. Soon, customers were taking the bags on vacation to add to the impromptu collection and the "Bags Around The World" exhibit was born.

If you've got a charge card, you've got a community! The nation's fourth largest department store chain **J.C. Penney Company, Inc.** creates special sales for its community of credit cardholders. A recent two-day sale offered J.C. Penney cardholders an extra 10% savings over and above the already reduced sale prices.

BUILD COMMUNITIES AROUND EDUCATION

Education is a smart community builder. The NMR Instruments Unit of Palo Alto, California–based **Varian Associates** used the Internet to create a worldwide community among the highly specialized group of scientists who use its nuclear magnetic resonance spectrometers. (The equipment is used to analyze molecular structures and can cost up to $25 million.) The "Virtual Customer Support Network" features an electronic newsletter and support services, as well as e-links to NMR employees and other customers.

General Electric Medical Systems (GEMS), a Wisconsin-based medical equipment manufacturer, created TiP-TV to engender loyalty among its hospital/clinic clientele. TiP, short for Training in Partnership, uses a television network to broadcast live and interactive training sessions that teach customers to use GEMS equipment as effectively as possible. This fee-based training qualifies toward hospital personnel's continuing education requirements and keeps GEMS close to its customers.

———————— ● ————————

The nation's oldest existing mail-order operation, **The Orvis Company, Inc.,** founded in 1856, shows customers how to get the most from its high-end fishing and hunting equipment with fly-fishing and hunting schools across the country. Orvis began teaching the sports in 1968 to ensure a steady stream of new customers; and since then, the schools have turned into a profit center all their own.

———————— ● ————————

Printing giant **Quad/Graphics** build its customer communities around free three-day educational seminars run annually in April and May. The $1.2 billion company calls the program "Camp Quad" and uses it to teach customers about new products and printing processes.

———————— ● ————————

The fast-growing community of do-it-yourselfers is always looking for good working advice and smart home center retailers, like the nation's 2nd largest home improvement superstore chain **Lowe's Companies.** Lowe's keeps its handy customers coming back by offering new home improvement projects and tool demonstrations each week. The clinics are free, and recently included such diverse topics as water heater installation, hanging wallpaper, organizing storage space, and Stanley tool and Troy-Bilt mower demonstrations.

———————— ● ————————

Goodwill is the one and only asset that competition cannot undersell or destroy.

—Marshall Field

*Four Ways to Grow
Profits from
Communities*

In their *Harvard Business
Review* article, Arthur
Armstrong and John
Hagel describe how on-
line communities con-
tribute to company
profitability:

1. Earn revenue by
   charging entry fees to
   join the community.

2. Earn revenue from the
   sale of the commu-
   nity's content.

3. Earn revenue from the
   sale of goods and ad-
   vertising.

4. Cut internal expenses
   by letting the commu-
   nity replace a more
   expensive operation—
   such as online vs.
   telephone support.

Communication parts and assemblies maker **AMP, Inc.** builds sales and brand recognition among the contractors that use its products with its Netconnect Design and Installation (NDI) program. NDI is a loyalty initiative that includes free training, co-op advertising, and a rebate on purchases to contractors AMP identifies as desirable partners. In return, the contractors use the $6 billion Harrisburg, Pennsylvania company's products and build AMP brand recognition among their customers.

————— ● —————

Winnipeg, Canada–based **Conviron's** customers add up to the largest group of users of controlled environment equipment in the world. The company built on that franchise by connecting those scientists into a network and fosters that network with conferences and on-line communication. Says CEO Richard Croft, "Stuff is flying around the world, and scientists are constantly moving around. We go to great lengths to see that they carry the knowledge of our products with them."

————— ● —————

The country's largest retailer of crafts supplies, Irving, Texas–based **Michaels Stores, Inc.,** makes sure its customers know how to use the 40,000 items it stocks by sponsoring its own free project demonstrations. These are often timed to coincide with holidays, like the two-hour program on a Saturday in mid-March, when customers learned how to "create a whimsical bunny centerpiece."

————— ● —————

General Nutrition Corp., the leading retailer of nutrition products, knows that its customers share a concern for good health and wellness. To keep that community coming into their chain, it recently ran an in-store seminar called

"A Lifetime of Health and Well-Being." Participants got samples, personal training tips, and refreshments along with lectures from specialists, including dentists, massage therapists, bodybuilders, and chiropractors. By creating a learning environment and making the store a clearinghouse for health services, GNC gives its customers a reason to stop in, even when they don't need a new supply of vitamins.

———— • ————

Franklin Covey Company's Franklin Planner family of products is the world's best-selling calendar system encompassing time management, goal setting, and planning. The Salt Lake City–based company, which merged with 7-Habits guru Stephen Covey's consulting firm, drives sales of planners and the annual refills through a never-ending series of educational seminars. The fee-based time management workshops teach new and existing customers how to use the products as organizational tools in their daily lives. Sign up and you also get a complimentary Planner and 30 days of technical support.

———— • ————

The Web is all about community. Vancouver, Washington–based **CompuPets** "sells Web-presence services to the pet industry." To help generate the traffic their site needs to build ad revenues, the company regularly hosts online seminars with pet breeders, veterinarians, and other experts, and offers chat rooms to keep surfers talking.

BORROW SOMEONE ELSE'S COMMUNITY

Communities of interest needn't be permanent or even focused directly on your product or

> Consumers are statistics. Customers are people.
>
> —STANLEY MARCUS

service in order to tap into their power. Take the time-honored bridal registry, a temporary community of interest centered around one wedding. Cranston, Rhode Island–based **Ross-Simons,** a retailer of tableware, jewelry, and collectibles, attracts these communities with a free bridal registry kit and a dedicated number, 1-800-82-BRIDE.

Once registered, the bride receives a $25 gift certificate toward her own shopping and free shipping on completion purchases. She also has access to bridal specialists who are available to help choose china, crystal, and silver as well as attendant gifts and favors. Of course, that is in addition to typical services, such as creating and tracking the gift wish list and making it available to her family and friends.

———————————●———————————

AAA Travel unveiled its take on the bridal registry with the AAA Travel Registry. The happy couple begins by putting a deposit on a honeymoon trip offered by the agency. In return, they receive registry cards that can be included in announcements and invitations sent to friends and family advising them how they can purchase the perfect wedding gift. Gift givers can contact the Registry and purchase gift certificates in any denomination toward the honeymoon trip. The AAA Travel Registry cards may also be used for other special events, such as anniversaries, birthdays, and graduations.

———————————●———————————

Mail-order giant **Eddie Bauer** knows you don't need to be a bride to attract your personal community of interest. So, now any customer can set up a gift registry on Eddie Bauer's Web site by providing their name, applicable sizes, and a list of all his or her preferred merchandise. Friends and family can log on anytime, look up the recipient and order the perfect gift, all from their PC.

———— • ————

J.C. Penney Company subscribes to the same philosophy with its Perfect Match Gift Registry program. Any and all J.C. Penney customers are invited to take advantage of the chain's hand-held scanners to create their own gift registry. The larger stores also have personal gift consultants to help customers make their choices. The gift registry is nationwide and includes a completion program.

———— • ————

Even **Microsoft** has boarded the registry train. Its Personal Computing "Gotta Have It" Gift Registry allows customers to create their own list of must-have software online and e-mail it to anyone they'd like.

———— • ————

Toy superstore chain **Toys 'R' Us** came up with a good twist on the bridal registry that answers the age-old question, "What do you want for Christmas?" Kids are loaned portable scanners that let them wander the store to build a computerized wish list by scanning the toys of their dreams. After the canvassing is done, a computerized list of the desired goods is generated and transmitted to all the chain's stores nationwide. Now, even distant relatives can give just the right gift.

———— • ————

Discount retailer **Target** keeps customers coming back with a similar scanner-based system for bridal and baby shower registries. Go to Target's customer service desk, sign up for Club Wedd or the Lullaby Club and you are on your way. As an added incentive, the Lullaby Club offers a 68-page gift guide, tote bag, and assorted coupons to those who register.

Ukrop's has turned extended families with new babies into a community of interest. Parents and grandparents of children under age two are eligible to join Ukrop's Baby Club. Baby Club members receive a $10 gift certificate rebate for every $100 spent on baby products at the store. They also receive quarterly newsletters, coupons on sponsors' products and special sweepstakes entries. The sponsors include Gerber, Drypers Diapers, Johnson & Johnson, and American Greetings, among others.

Can you build a temporary community around an event? Virginia's **Colonial Downs** racetrack did with its "Kentucky Derby Bash." The track, which wasn't running any of its own races on Derby Day, offered free admission, racing programs, and prize drawings throughout the day. And, brought in race fans to generate OTB (off-track betting) revenue.

Norfolk, Virginia's **Sheraton Waterside** capitalized on the Star Wars mania with a package including advance tickets to the movie, a gift certificate for theater snacks, and a one-night stay in the hotel—starting at $99.

How will it do? The hotel created a similar deal when *The Phantom of the Opera* came to town, and sold over 600 packages.

Toys 'R' Us knows well what kind of business Star Wars–branded toys generate. So, in its first-ever fit of Midnight Madness, the entire chain opened at 12:01 A.M. on the toys' release date to grab the first customers.

Borders Group Inc. book chain isn't one to miss a party. It invited their customers to "Join

---

Local theaters have been informed which cinemas will have the [new Star Wars] film on its opening date, but they have not been given permission—from director George Lucas, who controls every aspect of the film's marketing strategy—to announce it. When advance tickets go on sale, probably May 12, it is expected to touch off a frenzy.

—*DAILY PRESS,* MAY 2, 1999

in on some intergalactic fun with our Star Wars Party at Borders! We'll partake of some tasty snacks, play a trivia game, hold Chewbacca and Darth Vader impersonation contests, and end the evening with fun light saber duels! Remember to come dressed up as your favorite Star Wars character, 'cause we're giving away lots of cool prizes! Don't miss out!" (With permission of Lucasfilms, of course.)

———————●———————

Direct marketer **Lands' End, Inc.** borrows communities of interest through its sponsorships of modern adventurers. In 1997, it backed the Carter Viking ship voyage that sought to prove that the Vikings were able to reach North America centuries before Columbus. In 1998, it sponsored a team on the 1,100-mile Iditarod Trail Sled Dog Race. The progress of each journey was featured on the company's Web site and attracted plenty of positive attention.

———————●———————

Colonial Williamsburg (CW) created a community of ambassadors with its "Good Neighbor" program. Residents of the city of Williamsburg get free admission to all of the historic sites and free use of CW's bus service. In addition, there is a variety of special pricing, including 40 to 50% discounts on up to 10 guest passes per year; a dedicated reservation telephone number for area restaurants and taverns; and a 25% discount on events. How do you earn revenue when you give away admissions? Good Neighbors bring a steady stream of their guests to the historic area and those admissions are paid.

Historic sites close to CW immediately saw the value of the community addressed by the Good Neighbor program and joined up, too.

> Every business can indeed be a stage for offering economic experiences. Whether selling to consumers or customers, firms must recognize that goods and services are no longer enough; customers now want experiences.
>
> —B. Joseph Pine and James Gilmore in *The Experience Economy*

You can close more business in two months by becoming interested in other people than you can in two years by trying to get people interested in you.

—DALE CARNEGIE

The Good Neighbor pass, and all CW admissions, include free admission to the **Jamestown Settlement** and the **Yorktown Victory Center.**

———●———

Belle Plaine, Minnesota–based **Excelsior-Henderson** was so impressed with Harley-Davidson's community of loyal customers, it joined the group to sell its version of the long-gone, highly collectable Indian motorcycle. The company set up at the annual Harley rally in Sturgis, South Dakota, to introduce their product and are borrowing liberally from the H-D model. "We're fostering the Excelsior-Henderson lifestyle," company co-founder Dan Hanlon told *Inc.* magazine in November 1997.

———●———

Netpulse, a maker of the computerized monitors found on exercise equipment in gyms, borrowed its *customers' customer community* to build sales. Here's how it works: If your gym has a Netpulse-equipped exercise bike, you can join Netpulse's free Mile-a-Minute Program. Cycle for 500 minutes and Netpulse will send you a 500-mile frequent flyer voucher, good on either American Airlines or United Airlines. What's in it for Netpulse? Exercise equipment with Netpulse monitors generate business for the gyms, gyms generate business for equipment makers, and equipment makers buy Netpulse.

———●———

Cleveland, Ohio's **Medic Discount Drugstores** chain borrows the employee communities of its corporate neighbors to grow repeat business. Companies and their employees are invited to join the free Medic Value Prescription (MVP) Plan. On enrollment, employees receive personalized MVP cards for themselves and any immediate family members, which entitle them to 30% to 50% savings on generic prescriptions and Medic brand products, as well as a 10% discount on home health-care products.

———————•———————

Delta Air Lines and **American Express** teamed up to build a community for female business travelers with their Executive Woman's Travel Network. A fine mix of content and incentive, the Network is based online. It offers members resources, such as travel advisories and city profiles, and plenty of perks—starting with savings certificates for Delta flights for signing up. There is also a well-focused bundle of partner offers, such as discounts from Canyon Ranch Health Resorts, Royal Caribbean Cruise Line, Radisson, and others.

———————•———————

Found a community of interest, but don't have a product or service for it? Invent one. The **Bank of New Castle** teamed up with **Novus** to offer an affinity card with enormous appeal to the nation's many home gardeners. Using the Yard Card earns points that can be redeemed for catalog merchandise aimed at the devotees of the backyard, such as Black & Decker tools and Meadowcraft outdoor furniture.

———————•———————

Efax.com tapped into the community of folks that have e-mail but not fax machines to create its business model. Sign up at the company's Web site, and you are given a telephone number to receive faxes. When a fax arrives, Efax turns it into an e-mail and sends it to you. All for free. How does Efax make money? It

Monopolies Collapse

Even when your customers have little alternative but to come to you (think utilities and cable, for example), you better not take them for granted. Treat them like "hostages" and when the situation changes, they may well turn into "terrorists," according to Thomas Jones and W. Earl Sasser, Jr.

sells advertising that is shown on the "envelope" in which your fax arrives. Sound like a losing proposition? Efax pulled in 300,000 subscribers in its first two months of business.

———— ● ————

Even in a town that attracts over a million tourists per year, Williamsburg's **Fort Magruder Inn** needs to keep its local clientele coming back. It reached out for the resident community during the annual February tourist lull with its "License to Please" lunch buffet promotion. Simply flash a current Virginia driver's license, and walk away with a 25% discount from the standard price, or $5.95 instead of $7.95.

———— ● ————

Another of our local eateries, **Hayashi Japanese Restaurant,** targets specific communities by offering different discounts on various weeknights. Monday is Hospitality Night when all employees of hotels or hospitality-related businesses receive a 15% discount off their bill. Tuesday is William and Mary Night when students and faculty of the college receive 15% off their entire bill. Wednesday night is for Senior Citizens who receive 15% off their bills.

———— ● ————

Miami, Florida's **AvMed Health Plan** created a community around the senior citizens enrolled in its medical plans. The HMO's 1-to-1 Program reaches out to its older clients with a selection of free services, including contacts with volunteers to help with errands and chores, personalized health risk assessments, and (when indicated) referrals to outside health or social service agencies. It also raised the organization's retention rate among seniors.

———— ● ————

Hecht's department stores give seniors a good reason to come to the store with an annual one-day sale. On that day, seniors get an extra 10% discount on everything in the store. Says the chain, "If you're 55 years of age or older, take advantage of an extra 10% savings on any charge or cash purchase. Just show proof of age to any Sales Associate."

———————— ● ————————

The **Target Stores** discount chain has been reaching out to senior citizens with a 25-year holiday tradition. Each December, every Target store dedicates one morning to a shopping party for seniors. You can't get in unless you are a senior and the party includes complimentary entertainment, food, and gift wrapping.

———————— ● ————————

Just in case you still haven't gotten the spark that you need to tap into your own community of interest, prepare to be inspired by the keep-your-customers-coming-back virtuosity of Chicago cab driver **Ellis Miller.** Miller attracts repeat business on his run to and from the airport by playing matchmaker for his riders. Riders complete a "love resume" and review an in-cab portfolio of potential mates. In the event of a match, the driver arranges the date. It turned out to be such a good idea that Ellis added a fee for the service.

If a 200,000-member HMO, with an average premium of $120 per month, has 8% of its customer defect per year, the loss in annual revenue is close to $24 million.

—HSM GROUP
WHITE PAPER

STAND BEHIND YOUR WORK

One word: Trust! Trust is a critical factor in building repeat business. Think of it as a simple two-step process:

Step 1 in building trusting relationships with customers is delivering what you promise—the exact products and services at the price and time agreed upon.

Step 2 kicks in if (or more accurately, when) you break the promise you made in Step 1. The "when" is not meant as an insult. It is the practical recognition of all that is unforeseen. Products are sometimes flawed; computers crash; people make errors. Mistakes happen, so plan ahead for how to make things right again.

In any case, it's a pretty good bet that when a company stands behind its work, the customers will stand behind the company. Guarantees and warranties are two of the most widely used and easily recognized ways to show customers that you are confident in your work and are ready to support their relationship with your company. Guarantees and warranties take many forms, but we found that almost all fall into one of three categories: product, service, and price.

Product warranties are commonplace these days; they are perhaps the most familiar to consumers and are expected on just about all products. The challenge today is to find creative ways to use warranties to differentiate your company from your competitors and keep customers coming back because they are sure of getting a high-quality product.

Customers are often more worried about purchasing services than products. After all, defects in service are often subjectively defined and outcomes are not always predictable. All the more reason to stand behind your services.

Sometimes the most important guarantee you can offer customers is that they are receiving the best price. Price guarantees give customers the confidence to make their purchases immediately and reduce a company's risk of losing sales while customers go shopping for lower costs at a competitor's business. Further, price is usually one of the most important considerations in making a purchase. Guarantee the price and loyal customers will always know that they can buy from you without remorse.

STAND BEHIND YOUR PRODUCT

Nobody doesn't like the **Coach Leatherware Company,** a subsidiary of the Sara Lee Corporation. Ask customers why they are willing to pay a premium for the company's goods, and the lifelong warranty is sure to come up. The company brands each of its expensive handbags and other leather goods with its own unique serial number. Fill out the warranty card, return it to Coach, and the company will repair the product free of charge (except for a small shipping charge) for as long as you own it.

————— • —————

Hartmann, which has been making high-quality, handcrafted leather goods for over 120 years, also enjoys a reputation for standing behind its product. It guarantees all products to be free from defects for the life of the product. In addition, items that have deteriorated due to normal wear and tear can be returned to Hartmann at any time for repair. If, after inspection, the company determines that there is a charge for the service, Hartmann will call the customer with a quote within five to seven days.

————— • —————

Fine men's footwear maker **Allen-Edmunds** takes a stand on the quality of its workmanship. Starting in 1991, it extended the life of its shoes with its recrafting service. The recrafting process turns worn wingtips into new ones for a fraction of the cost of buying a new pair, and the company offers four economical repair packages to customers. The company even pays the cost of getting the shoes in for recrafting. Post-paid shoe bags are available from the dealer or a call to the toll-free number. "Imagine that," says president of the 77-year-old company, John Stollenwerk, "a shoe company that retains its shine."

————— • —————

We particularly liked the wording of the full-refund guarantee **Worth** magazine uses to attract repeat business: "If *Worth* doesn't help improve your net worth during your renewal year, just tell us and we'll refund your money in full." Now that's putting your money where your magazine is.

————— • —————

> One bad experience and poof . . . customers are history. Sure, you can replace them—but at five times the cost.
>
> —PAAVO HANNINEN,
> DIRECTOR AT THE
> SMALL BUSINESS
> DEVELOPMENT CENTER,
> UNIVERSITY OF ALABAMA

It's all the more important that mail-order companies stand behind their products. After all, they ask customers to buy products before they can actually touch, see, and in the case of **Omaha Steaks,** taste them. No worries with this company, however. Customers who are not completely satisfied with their order get a replacement or a full refund, whichever they prefer.

———— • ————

Plow & Hearth, a direct marketer selling "Products for Country Living," offers the "Spirit of Country Living 100% Guarantee." Any item purchased from the company may be returned for any reason at any time if the buyer is not 100% satisfied. Customers may return the item for exchange or full refund.

By the way, the cataloger also offers price protection. Find the same merchandise cheaper somewhere else and the company promises to refund the difference.

———— • ————

Smith & Hawken, a retailer of everything one needs to garden in high style, makes its promises in plain English. If customers are "less than pleased" with any item, the company "will cheerfully accept it for an exchange or refund of the full price of the merchandise." Further, if in the *customer's* opinion "a product fails to hold up under normal use for a reasonable period of time," Smith & Hawken will replace the item. And, for good measure, "if you simply decide you don't want the merchandise, please return it within six months."

———— • ————

Kids love stickers, and Nevada's **Vending Supply, Inc.** makes and sells millions of them each year through its customers' vending machines. Customer tastes change quickly in this market, so Vending Supply encourages its vending machine owners to try out the latest, but as-yet unproven, designs by guaranteeing that the owners would not lose money on them. In an interview for *Management Review,* CEO Robert Winquist said, "We improved our service to vendors themselves, ultimately offer[ing] a 100% refund policy, unthinkable in this business."

———— ● ————

You should be able to play rough with a sports watch, so Swiss watchmaker **Burett** offers a lifetime warranty on its high-end Burett 2002 watch. Repairs are free with a copy of the sales receipt. For those customers who abuse the watch beyond all reason, the company will be happy to offer an estimate for the service after they receive it.

———— ● ————

Book lovers are sure to be familiar with Delray Beach, Florida–based **Levenger, Inc.,** which sells "Tools for Serious Readers" through catalogs and its retail store. From the start, the company wanted to be sure its customers were completely satisfied and so created a full-refund policy that includes return shipping costs.

———— ● ————

Palantine, Illinois–based **Weber-Stephen Products Company** shows its commitment to the quality of its outdoor barbecues with a warranty program that includes a 45-day money-back guarantee and a 25-year limited warranty. The company went a step further, creating 1-800-GRILL-OUT (a hotline for grilling tips) and a toll-free customer-service number for problems.

———— ● ————

Competing with the myriad of office-supply superstores popping up around the country isn't easy, but Ottawa, Illinois–based **Reliable Corporation** backs up its catalog operation with an unconditional guarantee. Anything purchased from this subsidiary of Boise Cascade is subject to a 30-day free trial. If not satisfied, the company refunds the purchase price and pays for the return shipping.

———— ● ————

Like most prescription medication, the cholesterol-reducing drug Zocor is expensive. But, it differs from other prescription remedies because the nation's largest pharmaceutical company, **Merck & Co., Inc.,** has decided to back up its effectiveness with a "Get-to-Goal Guarantee." Merck will give customers (or their insurance companies) their money back, if they use Zocor for 30 days and it doesn't work.

———— ● ————

Bradford, Pennsylvania–based **Zippo Manufacturing Company** is the only remaining American maker of refillable lighters. Maybe that's because it prides itself on the fact that none of its customers has ever spent any money repairing its products—since 1933. Other than the exterior finish, every part of a Zippo lighter is guaranteed for life. "It works or we fix it free," declares the company. Customers take them up on this guarantee to the tune of 1,000 lighters per day, most of them needing only a new hinge. Even if customers send the lighter with money for postage or repairs, the Zippo Repair Clinic returns the money with the restored lighter.

———— ● ————

Sometimes a lifetime guarantee is simply the price of admission to a market. Several generations of hand tool buyers are familiar with **Sears, Roebuck and Company's** Craftsman brand tools. Break a Craftsman hand tool, even those that get notoriously heavy use such as utility knives and aluminum snips, and Sears will replace it with a new one—no charge.

———— • ————

A subsidiary of the Lowe's Companies, **LF Corporation** matched that with its KOBALT brand tools. The company offers a simple guarantee: The tools will work forever. And, just in case they don't, customers can return the tool to the place of purchase for a free replacement . . . no questions asked.

———— • ————

Atlanta-based **The Home Depot, Inc.** knew what it had to do to launch its Husky brand tool line. If a Husky tool ever breaks, Home Depot will replace it free of charge.

The largest do-it-yourself chain, Home Depot, extends its tool guarantee to merchandise throughout its stores. As founders Bernie Marcus and Arthur Blank say in their book *Built from Scratch*, "The key to our no-holds-barred return policy is that people talk about it. It gets them hooked; they know they can never make a bad purchase at The Home Depot, because we don't ever want to give them a reason not to come back."

———— • ————

Lowe's Companies' Lowe's Home Improvement Warehouse lawn and garden departments keep customers coming back with their "One Year Plant Guarantee." Any tree, shrub, and houseplant purchased from Lowe's that does not live for one year will be replaced free of charge. And, no lugging around dead trees; the only evidence customers need is the original receipt.

———— • ————

> No sale is really complete until the product is worn out and the customer is satisfied.
>
> —LEON (L. L.) BEAN

Firm and clear are the two hallmarks of a strong guarantee. Listen to the world's largest postage meter maker **Pitney Bowes, Inc.:** "This five-year guarantee means that if you are not satisfied with the performance of this product, Pitney Bowes will promptly replace it at our expense. If we provide a replacement product and it does not fully perform according to specifications, we will promptly give you a full refund. You will have no concerns after you acquire this product. Our customer satisfaction guarantee means that your problems are our problems and will be resolved promptly. In short, it means no excuses from Pitney Bowes."

———— • ————

Land's End, Inc.'s guarantee is even simpler: "If you are not completely satisfied with any item you buy from us, at any time during your use of it, return it, and we will refund your full purchase price."

Land's End doesn't just stand behind its products; it also stands behind its service. During the 1997 UPS strike that crippled the direct marketers around the country, the company quickly created a shipping partnership with the U.S. Postal Office to make sure that the 40,000-odd orders shipped each day still arrived at customers' doors in good time. Because the company was unable to fulfill most rush shipping requests, it offered free shipping instead.

———— • ————

Lebanon, Ohio–based **Frontgate's** catalogs are filled with luxuries designed for "Enhancing your life at home." They include pool toys, leather-bound remote control boxes, and state-of-the-art personal electronics. The cataloger keeps customers coming back with two confidence-builders.

When product quality is similar, it's customer service that tips the scale in your favor.

—Michael Smith, president of Land's End in *Customer Service*

First, the company offers the "395 Day Signature Guarantee," a creative extension that means customers can live with their purchases for a full 13 months before deciding whether or not they'd like to keep them. Then, Frontgate ups the ante with price protection. Customers may request a refund of the price difference for any product sold for less in another catalog, including taxes and shipping. Price protection is available for 90 days after purchase.

———— ● ————

Those companies that are best at standing behind their work know that the mishaps that are bound to occur occasionally are really opportunities to build customer loyalty in disguise. Consider **The Popcorn Factory's** response to a customer's complaint. The direct seller of popcorn and a catalog full of related products quickly responded to a phone call about a stale product. The day after the call, the customer received a letter of apology along with two new tins of fresh popcorn.

———— ● ————

When **Volkswagen Group** introduced the New Beetle, it harbored a wiring bug that could cause fires. The company not only fixed the bug; it authorized dealers to spend $100 per owner to apologize for the inconvenience. "We were hoping they would buy them flowers, or buy them lunch, or maybe, if it was New York, give them a cab ride," Volkswagen's Tony Fouladpour told the *New Yorker*. "But we know some of the dealers just gave them the cash."

———— ● ————

Personal experience: After wearing a **J. Crew** barn jacket for over a year and finding it impossible to keep clean, we finally called the company for advice. "Are you unhappy with

Leonard Berry's Three Rules of Service Recovery

1. Do it right the first time.

2. Fix it if it fails.

3. Remember: There are no third chances.

your purchase?" asked the rep. Our "yes" produced a wholly unexpected response. The company *asked us* to send the jacket back for a full refund and apologized for the inconvenience. We've been customers ever since.

———— ● ————

Another: We bought a pair of **Pottery Barn** curtains that looked great in the catalog, but not so good at home. We figured we could work around them, but months passed and we couldn't. Finally, we called the company and told a service rep the story. After a very short period of deliberation, she assured us that they wanted us to be happy with their curtains and authorized an exchange. Customers ever since.

———— ● ————

One more: Living in Cleveland, we liked to eat at the **Cooker Bar & Grille,** a regional chain serving a wide-range of American specialties. Every meal, a manager stops by the table and asks how it was. One night, we looked at our now-empty plates and mentioned that the meatloaf was okay, but not quite as tasty as usual. It came right off the bill. If only they'd open a location in Virginia.

———— ● ————

Not all employees are as amenable: **Marshall Fields,** founder of the Chicago-based department store chain, once came upon an employee arguing with a customer.

"What are you doing here?" Field demanded.

"I'm settling a complaint," came back the reply.

"No, you're not," said Field. "Give the lady what she wants." And, that phrase became the chain's motto.

———— ● ————

Century Furniture in Hickory, North Carolina, builds quality furniture and it made its attitude toward its workmanship clear in this

Never underestimate the power of an irate customer.

—Joel Ross

incident: After six moves and 16 years, when one of the hinges on a Century armoire finally gave up the fight, friends of ours say the company quickly responded with a personal note containing two identical replacement hinges— one extra just in case. Guess what brand of furniture they recommend?

———— • ————

We had a similar experience when we lost the rubber straps that secure our bicycles to the **Rhode Gear** 2-Bike Shuttle on our car. The one-year limited warranty was long expired and anyway, the defect was in the owner's memory. We couldn't buy replacements, however. The customer service rep insisted on sending the four replacement straps, and four extras, without charge. Which racks do you think we recommend?

———— • ————

Buy fiber-optic cabling from Lexington, South Carolina–based **Pirelli Cable Corporation,** and it comes along with the company's "Twenty-four By Seven" emergency response teams. Knowing that cable mishaps can translate to vital communication outages, Pirelli established a toll-free number that generates urgent messages to team members no matter where they are. Once a team member takes the call, that person manages the response from start to finish.

———— • ————

Greenville, South Carolina's **Hartness International** backs up its product guarantees with a video response system to cut the downtime if its high-volume packing machines (that load bottles and jars into cartons) stop running. Installed at the customer's site, the system includes a wireless camera, a remote control, and a monitor, and allows Hartness to conduct

> Customers don't want their money back; they want a product that works properly.
>
> —Dan Burton,
> business writer

remote repair sessions that solve up to 80% of their service problems.

———●———

Bicycle retailer **BikeBeat** makes this promise: "All bikes are professionally assembled at Bike-Beat and come with a lifetime warranty and service protection." The free guarantee not only saves customers money, but also gets them back into the shop anytime they need repairs.

———●———

Colorado-based **Bella Luna Books** offers a unique guarantee on the modern first editions it sells to collectors through its catalog. Not only do they extend a lifetime guarantee to their customers; they further extend it to their customers' heirs. When it comes time to sell any book purchased from Bella Luna, the bookseller will buy it back at the full purchase price or current wholesale value, whichever is higher. How's that for standing behind your product and your price!

STAND BEHIND YOUR SERVICE

Service guarantees are as important as product guarantees. For golfers who want to spend their time on the course instead of shopping for equipment, customer service champion **Nordstrom** department stores marketed Callaway Golf shoes with a unique guarantee. At the start of the 1998 golf season, Nordstrom assured its customers it would have all common sizes of "Maximus" spikeless golf shoes in stock. If not, they were special ordered and given to the customer for free. Nordstrom's promise: "These shoes, these sizes, or they're free."

———●———

Bloomingdale's made sure that it didn't ruin its catalog customers' Thanksgiving dinners with this guarantee: Orders for fine china sporting the "place-setting" logo and placed by November 9th were guaranteed to be in customers' homes by Thanksgiving or that merchandise was free.

———— • ————

Truth in advertising legislation requires that most sales be backed up with guarantees in the form of rain checks, but **Sears, Roebuck and Co.** goes a step further. If customers don't want to return to the store to use a rain check, they may purchase a "substitute item at the same percentage discount if the [out-of-stock] item was reduced" or "an equal or better item at the advertised price if the item was not reduced."

———— • ————

One more in the Who-says-there's-no-free-lunch? department: At the Plano, Texas–based **Bennigan's** restaurant chain, if your weekday lunch isn't on the table in 15 minutes, it's free. And, don't worry about time keeping; your server sets a timer right on the table as the order is placed. We know customers who go to Bennigan's for lunch just to try to beat the clock.

———— • ————

There are a lot of places to rent videos these days, but it often seems like weeks go by before you can find one that has a single copy left of that popular new release. Video rental chain behemoth **Blockbuster Video,** with over 5,000 stores in more than 20 countries, makes a strong play for customer loyalty with a unique guarantee. Each week the company creates a list of popular recent releases; and if one isn't available for rent when you want it, Blockbuster will give you the rental for free when the movie comes back in.

———— • ————

> **The critical element in selling a service comes in providing support after the sale, because, unlike other types of marketing, the customer can't really try the product until he's already bought it.**
>
> —KAY KNIGHT CLARKE, PRESIDENT OF TEMPLETON, INC.

Total Trust requires going beyond the realm of customer satisfaction and customer delight, to become a company that your customers believe will always act in their best interest. Customer trust is the belief, backed by experience, that your organization—and your employees—will be fair, reliable, competent and ethical in all dealings."

—Christopher Hart,
University of Michigan
professor and author of
Extraordinary Guarantees
in *President*

London-based advertising agency **Publicis Technology** makes the intangible tangible with an unusual fee structure that is helping it break into the U.S. market. Publicis knows that if its ad campaigns are successful, its customers' products or services will garner a larger share of the market, which in turn should increase the client firm's stock price. So, as one way to guarantee their bottom-line performance, Publicis bases 10 to 15% of its fee on fluctuations in the client's stock price. Either way, they share their customer's fate.

———— • ————

Some of the lushest, greenest lawns in our town are kept that way by **Grass Roots of Virginia, LLC.** The company seeds, feeds, and de-weeds its customers' lawns on a regular schedule—and stands behind its service. Service calls are provided at no additional cost and homeowners are quickly met on site by a pro if green fades to brown. Conditions related to the company's treatments are fixed free of charge and those beyond the usual service are quickly quoted.

———— • ————

National pest control chain **Terminex International** guarantees you won't be bugged when you sign up for regular-scheduled maintenance. If bugs come back between visits, so will the company, at no extra charge.

———— • ————

FedEx revolutionized the industry with its overnight service and set the standard for performance with its service guarantees. It makes two separate and distinct money-back guarantees on each and every package it ships. The first guarantees the date and the time of delivery and will refund the cost of shipment is your package is so much as a minute late. The second offers a money-back guarantee if FedEx cannot tell its customers the status of their packages within 30 minutes of the inquiry.

———— ● ————

United Parcel Service (UPS) recently raised the stakes for small package shippers by extending its delivery guarantees to all the packages it handles, including ground shipments. If any package in the continental U.S. or Canada arrives late, UPS refunds the shipping cost.

———— ● ————

Trucking company **Yellow Freight** used the same strategy for the heavy end of the overnight shipping market. The company's Exact Express Expedited Air & Ground Delivery takes packages over 70 pounds and ships them to their clients' exact specifications in terms of delivery date and hour of delivery if necessary. And, that service is fully guaranteed, too.

———— ● ————

Shippers aren't the only ones guaranteeing package delivery. When **Mail Boxes Etc.** (MBE) ships packages for its clients, they guarantee the safe arrival of the shipment or your money back. Recently, when a package shipped by the franchise arrived at its destination in damaged condition, MBE quickly sent a letter of apology to the customer who brought in the package, along with a check for the declared value of $100 and a refund of the entire shipping charge.

———— ● ————

Virginia-based custom builder **VanKniest, Inc.** provides a welcome relief from the seemingly endless stream of contractor horror stories, largely because owner John Kniest, Jr., stands behind the homes and commercial complexes his company constructs. Kniest responds to post-construction problems in person, inspecting and establishing the proper resolution with

Exceptional Service . . .
No Exceptions

—ROADWAY EXPRESS'
PROMISE TO CUSTOMERS

his customers, before dispatching workers to the site. The result is a top-flight reputation in a demanding, competitive market.

———— • ————

Personal experience: We took an inexpensive junket to **Caesar's Palace** in Las Vegas. We didn't expect luxury, but the room was directly above the hotel's trash bins and *they* looked a little cleaner than the room. We called the front desk, which readily agreed to a different room. Hours went by and no new room. We called the front desk again and in the blink of an eye, a bellhop was escorting us out of the low-rent district and high up into the hotel's newly renovated tower. He opened the door to a great room with a stunning view, a huge round bed (mirrored above, of course), and a black marble bath. It was a big step up.

———— • ————

New Brunswick, New Jersey's **Robert Wood Johnson University Hospital** (RWJ) has offered a money-back guarantee to their emergency patients. After experiencing delays so long that many emergency room patients simply walked out, RWJ reengineered its entire emergency care process. Now, if patients who enter the emergency room are not seen by a nurse in less than 15 minutes and a doctor in less than 30 minutes, the care the patient finally does receive is free.

———— • ————

Perhaps even more welcome, given the negative reputation of the cable TV industry, is **Cox Communications, Inc.'s** guarantee. Cox says if its installation crew is late to install a new service, that service will be installed for free. If its employees are late for a service call to an existing customer, the customer gets a $20 credit on the next month's bill.

———————— • ————————

Buy computer memory or a new hard drive at superstore chain **CompUSA,** and it may be worth it to let them do the installation, too. The stores offers their customers "upgrade installation in 24 hours or it's free."

———————— • ————————

The online economy promises to be a gold mine for credit card companies; after all, the checkout counters in cyberspace don't take checks or cash. To build its share of the market and give its cardholders the same sense of security they get in physical stores, **American Express** now guarantees that their customers will not be held responsible for unauthorized charges online.

American Express also protects nearly everything cardholders purchase. The company's Buyer's Assurance Plan automatically extends the product's original five-year or less warranty up to an additional year on products priced up to $10,000. And, the Purchase Protection Plan automatically protects eligible purchases from theft and accidental damage for 90 days from the date of purchase.

———————— • ————————

Sometimes it's nice to know they really are watching. **VISA's** Fraud Office routinely calls cardholders to verify unusual account activity. Of course, the practice is motivated by a good measure of self-interest and a need to quickly cancel stolen cards. But, it also gives customers a sense of security. Recently, when married cardholders we know triggered a call with almost simultaneous purchases on the East and West Coasts, they expressed appreciation for the service.

———————— • ————————

Forget about blaming your service provider the next time you ignore that page. **SkyTel**

Think your company doesn't make a lot of mistakes? Well, they add up fast. Here's what 99.9% perfection means (courtesy of ink):

- *22,000 checks deducted from the wrong bank accounts in an hour*
- *12 newborns handed over to the wrong parents in a day*
- *114,500 mismatched shoes shipped in a year*
- *14,208 defective computers shipped each year*
- *1,314 misconnected phone calls every minute*

Corporation has created SkyWord Plus, the first national paging service that guarantees that you will get all of your messages. If the call isn't completed, the company's system stores and resends it until it is.

————— ● —————

How does your company respond to service lapses? Torrance, California's **Quatrine Furniture** often has little control over the exact delivery dates of the special orders it places on behalf of its furniture and accessory customers. When a recent order to centuries-old Italian silk manufacturer, Fortuny Laboratories, went awry for an extended period, Quatrine contacted the customer with apologies, an estimated delivery date, and a glossy coffee-table book detailing the heritage of Fortuny and its products.

————— ● —————

Merry Maids knows that house and office cleaning can sometimes result in accidents and damaged property. When a ceramic statue was broken in one home, the cleaners brought the accident to the owner's attention, apologized, and offered to take it back to their home office where it would be replaced with a new one and delivered back. They also offered alternative solutions: to repair it to the customer's satisfaction or deduct the cash value of the item from their cleaning services. The owner chose replacement; and within a week, a new statue was delivered.

————— ● —————

Even the most fastidious credit card holders occasionally have disputes with some of the charges on their monthly Visa or MasterCard statements. Correcting such errors are the sole responsibility of the cardholder, even when the error is not—except at **National City Bank,** where the smaller of these disputes are quickly eliminated. For customers in good standing

If a company excels in making amends—that is, in recovering— when such failures occur, customers' faith in the company is not just restored, it is deepened.

—THOMAS JONES AND W. EARL SASSER, JR., DISCUSSING SERVICE IN *HARVARD BUSINESS REVIEW* with disputes under $25, National City simply and automatically removes the charge. No forms to fill out, no question of interest charges being levied, and no proof required other than a good customer's honest complaint.

————— • —————

Citibank credit card holders in good standing with disputes of $10 or less get the same service. When the customer service operators input the disputed charge information into their computers, the system kicks back a message to them that a credit has been automatically issued. The credit appears on the cardholder's next statement.

————— • —————

Sometimes even service recovery efforts get snakebit. In the face of a written complaint from a customer who could not locally resolve the problem of a new refrigerator sporting a defective door at the local store, the **Sears Merchandise Group** swung into action. Unable to make contact by telephone, Sears mailed the direct office phone number for National Customer Relations and asked the customer to call them. Not only did the call produce a fridge door that was not defective; it was attached to another new refrigerator that worked perfectly right from the start.

————— • —————

When the nation's largest home improvement chain **Home Depot** repeatedly booted its delivery and installation of $1,200 in custom wood blinds and couldn't seem to make it right, the store's District Manager took a different tack. He not only got the blinds delivered and installed; the entire order was free. Says the former irate customer, "I would definitely go back to Home Depot."

————— • —————

Is a single customer worth a high-dollar hit to the bottom line? T. Scott Gross, inventor of

Former Nordstrom exec and author of *Fabled Service* (Jossey-Bass, 1995) Betsey Sanders offers up these eye-openers about customer complaints:

- Only 4% of unhappy customers complain; the rest leave angry.

- For every customer complaint you hear, there are 26 you don't hear.

- If you resolve a complaint quickly, 96% of customers will come back.

- The average disgruntled customer tells nine other people. Thirteen percent tell more than 20 others.

Positively Outrageous Service, tells this story: When an order for a chainsaw part at a **Coast to Coast** store in Ridgecrest, California, never materialized the new manager picked out a new 14-inch Homelite saw and gave it to the customer—on the house. Later that same day, the customer returned and bought $1,200 in merchandise. In the following year, the same customer spent $4,000.

STAND BEHIND YOUR PRICE

The most impressive price guarantee we found popped up in the highly competitive market for home audio. The **Tweeter** retail chain keeps customers coming back with a unique twist. All receipts issued by Tweeter include the product price and purchaser's name and address. This information is fed into a product database that notifies the stores automatically if a competitor has offered a lower price on a product than its customers have already paid. The result: without any action on the part of the customer, the store issues a refund check for the difference and sends it directly to the customer.

———— • ————

Our local **Berkeley Cleaners** stands behind its own prices by standing by its competitors' prices. They honor their competitors' coupons. It's a smart move that keeps regular customers coming back instead of shopping around for the best price.

———— • ————

Carmaker **Saturn** made a name for itself by promising a different kind of car-buying experience. The sales staff is known for educating its prospective customers, but not pressuring them. And, there is no haggling over sticker

prices. All buyers know they've gotten the best price the dealership offers. The company is serious about that: When it lowered sticker prices on several models in late 1997, Saturn refunded some $7 million to car owners who had paid the original sticker price.

———— ● ————

Richfood Holding's Farm Fresh grocery chain keeps customers using its in-store pharmacy by making them confident that they have paid the lowest price possible. Fill the same prescription locally at a lower price within 30 days and you get a refund of 125% of the difference in price.

———— ● ————

Sears, Roebuck and Co.'s Tire America outlets don't think 125% is enough. Find a lower advertised price within 30 days and "you get double the difference back."

———— ● ————

Tired of seeing the companies you regularly do business with offer new customers better prices than they offer you? Cellular phone service provider **360° Communications** (now Alltel Corporation) must know the feeling, because when it recently offered new customers 30 minutes of local calling free per month for one year, it extended the same free local call program to its existing customers who were ready to renew contracts.

———— ● ————

Attention **Kmart** shoppers, the Troy, Michigan–based discount chain not only offers "low prices all the time," it guarantees "the lowest sale prices every time." It simply says: "If you find a price lower than Kmart, simply bring it to our attention and we will match the price for you."

———— ● ————

Four Steps to Resolving Customer Complaints

- Get the facts and record them.
- Agree on a resolution and schedule it.
- Solve the problem.
- Follow up.

Lowe's home centers go a step further in their price guarantee. If customers find a lower advertised price, they can bring the ad to Lowe's, who will match the price and throw in an additional 10% for their trouble. If the item is found at a lower price in a competitor's store rather than in an ad, Lowe's will call the competitor to verify the price and match it plus 10%.

———●———

Office Depot, the nation's largest office-supply chain, raises the bar with its 155% Low Price Guarantee. If a local competitor advertises an identical item for less, customers who advise Office Depot within seven days receive the lower price plus 55% of the difference, up to a maximum of $55.

———●———

Now, if only they would do that for home mortgages. They did: Mortgage your house through Fairfax, Virginia's **Service Saver Finance** and refinance when the rates drop without paying fees or reapplying. When rates drop a half-percentage point and you've been paying your mortgage on time for at least 12 months, you can refinance on request—no new appraisals, no income or credit checks, just a lower rate mortgage.

———●———

So, why not make it automatic? They did: San Diego–based **City Line Mortgage** has come up with the "automatic rate reduction loan." This ingenious mortgage vehicle automatically refinances itself when the going rate for your fixed mortgage drops 1/2% below the rate you borrowed at—without any closing costs (provided the holder pays on time for at least 12 months and is financially stable). The automatic refinancing helps the lender retain about 95% of their current mortgage customers.

––––––– • –––––––

One of the many ways **Ukrop's Super Markets** keeps its customers coming back is to assure them they are getting the lowest prices along with great selection and legendary customer service. Ukrop's encourages customers to "take the Ukrop's pricing challenge" to find lower prices at competitors. This is no random challenge: First, customers buy at least 40 items at Ukrop's using their Valued Customer (UVC) card. Then, within a week, they must take their receipts to any competing grocer and compare prices on identical items, writing the competitors' prices directly on the Ukrop's receipt. What do you get for your trouble? When you mail the receipt to Ukrop's, the grocer will send back a $15 Ukrop's gift certificate; and if the Ukrop's bill is higher, double the difference of the total grocery bill.

––––––– • –––––––

Sneaker superstore **Just For Feet** offers its own "Low Price Guarantee." If its prices are beat in any local advertisement, the store will match the price.

––––––– • –––––––

Personal experience: We bought linens from **Bloomingdale's By Mail** and a couple of months later, here comes the new catalog with a 20% price reduction on the same items—a savings of several hundred dollars. We ruefully told a service rep the story the next time we bought from the company. A short wait on hold produced a credit for the full amount. Customers for life.

––––––– • –––––––

Branford, Connecticut–based bicycle shop **Zane's Cycles** puts it all together with a host of guarantees designed to keep its customers out of the sporting goods superstores. They include a price guarantee that there isn't a lower price in the state, a free lifetime service warranty covering all repairs; giving customers any item that costs less than a dollar for free; and, a no-receipt-required return policy for all items in the store's stock database.

GIVE IN ORDER TO RECEIVE

We've all heard the admonition that "It's better to give than it is to receive." Roughly two-thirds of American adults apparently agree with the statement since that's how many of us donate time and money to charitable activities each year.

Businesses are as philanthropically active as individuals. In 1996, corporate America gave away something on the order of $8.5 billion, according to the AAFRC Trust for Philanthropy. Based on this figure, it would seem that the idea of giving is not bad business.

The late Robert Goizueta, much-respected chairman of Coca-Cola Company, said it this way in a 1994 speech: "There are plenty of examples of business doing the right thing because they know it is the best thing for their long-term success."

If two-thirds of your customers care about more than business alone, you'd better too. Understanding that customers care about the world in which they live and supporting their concerns is a wonderful way to build loyal relationships and do good at the same time.

––––––––––––– • –––––––––––––

San Francisco–based **Working Assets Funding Service** created a business model around the idea of philanthropy. It competes in the

overcrowded credit card market by appealing to socially responsible consumers. The company donates a nickel of each customer's monthly charges to select nonprofit organizations.

The strategy has proven so popular that the company also offers long-distance telephone services based on the same principle of social responsibility. Sign up for the service and 10% of your monthly long-distance bill goes to a short list of good causes. Add to the payment and the company will automatically send the difference to its 50 designated charities.

Those nickels, and other corporate giving, add up. Since 1985, the company has given $16 million to nonprofits.

———— • ————

Marietta, Georgia's **Health Education Retirement Organization** just launched a new cash card called HERO. Purchases made on HERO generate a rebate that goes into a trust account in the customer's name. These accounts are periodically split and dispersed to pre-chosen charities and into designated savings vehicles for the customer, such as stocks, mutual funds, and savings bonds. In this way, the HERO card provides automatic savings along with tax-deductible donations.

———— • ————

Online marketer **CyberGold** gives its customers a small payment for browsing the advertising and promotions on its Web site. For surfers who see the bigger picture, CyberGold allows the option of donating these fees to several charitable organizations, such as the National Kidney Foundation and the Hereditary Disease Foundation.

———— • ————

Act locally . . . Milwaukee-based independent **Harry W. Schwartz Booksellers** created

If you want to lift yourself up, lift up someone else.

—Booker T. Washington

Schwartz Gives Back (SGB) to support its community. Customers joining SGB choose their favorite charity from a list of local organizations. Whenever the member makes a purchase, their nonprofit receives 1% of the total. SGB customers also receive regular promotional mailings complete with money-saving coupons for books.

———————— • ————————

Seattle-based insurer **SAFECO** recently joined with Seattle Habitat for Humanity to build a home for a low-income family. SAFECO employees kicked in the labor.

———————— • ————————

Warrendale, Pennsylvania's **Mitsubishi Electric Power Products, Inc.** created the annual "Tour de Sewickley" to support The Early Learning Institute, serving children with disabilities. The 60-, 30-, and 5-mile bike rides through Western Pennsylvania attract over 700 riders; and over the last six years, raised $150,000 for the Institute.

———————— • ————————

In Virginia, **Foot Locker** recently teamed up with **Ukrop's Super Markets** to fund Operation Gun Drive. The program paid cash for switchblades and guns from anyone age 16 and over willing to turn them in. The cash was collected by the Essex Village Community Church and Outreach Center, and Ukrop's matched every $1,000 collected for the program. Foot Locker donated store gift certificates, which were used in lieu of cash for anyone under 16 turning in weapons.

———————— • ————————

The **Freedom Ford Hampton** car dealership sponsored the transformation of a plot of vacant land at a local elementary school into a garden, complete with herbs, vegetables, and

The high destiny of the individual is to serve rather than to rule. . . .

—ALBERT EINSTEIN

fruit trees. Employees spent a Saturday working on the project with parents, students, and staff; and other local merchants helped with merchandise and supplies.

———— • ————

"Local" for **Southwest Airlines Company** is every community it serves. Each holiday season, the company runs its 'Home for the Holidays' program, which flies senior citizens who can't afford a ticket to their families. Home for the Holidays has run for 18 years and thousands of senior citizens have received free flights.

———— • ————

Think globally . . . After Hurricane Mitch, all 12 **Peace Frogs** T-shirt shops collected nonperishable food items for the Red Cross, which in turn sent the food to Central America. Customers who brought in food donations got 10% off their store purchases in return.

———— • ————

San Mateo, California–based Internet direct marketer, **Make It So, Inc.,** provides customers a similar incentive to buy computers and other merchandise through their Web site. Log on to ClubMail, choose from the list of children's charities shown, and every time you make a purchase, 1% of the sale goes to the selected charities. As of November 1998, the small business had sent off over $9,000 to nonprofits.

———— • ————

What kid wouldn't want to go to Disneyland for the holidays? Since 1995, **Kintetsu International Express (U.S.A.), Inc.** has been making sure underprivileged children and teenagers in Los Angeles area get that experience with its annual "Early Christmas Party at Disneyland." Here's how it works: Travel company Kintetsu charters Disneyland for one night every December as part of a tourism package, which attracts about 4,000 to 5,000 paying customers. It also invites over 1,000 children of LA's kids—on the house.

————————●————————

American Airlines makes sure its air miles get put to charitable use with the AAdvantage Fund Raising program. American provides its own fund-raising consultants free of charge to help the nonprofits come up with ways to incorporate the carrier's frequent flyer miles as incentives in their campaigns. Groups as diverse as the National Kidney Foundation and the Library Foundation of Los Angeles have taken "AAdvantage" of the program.

————————●————————

New Jersey's **Warner-Lambert Company** recently supported the World Journey of Hope '99, a global effort to provide reconstructive facial surgeries to people who cannot otherwise afford the procedures. For one week, the $8 billion company donated $1 for every participating product—including such popular brands as Listerine, Benadryl, Sudafed, Efferdent, and Schick—that customers purchased.

————————●————————

There is nothing inherently wrong with linking philanthropy and marketing. For decades, the **Campbell Soup Company** has been marketing to families and to children with such memorable characters as the Campbell's Soup Kids. Now, when you go into participating schools, you will see 4-foot-tall Campbell's Soup cans. The cans are the collection bins for proofs-of-purchase from Campbell's products. Schools that collect enough get free computers from the folks that brought you M'mmm Good!

————————●————————

Consumer food product giant **General Mills, Inc.** kept customers buying their Yoplait brand

If you don't care, your customer never will.

—Marlene Blaszczyk
Parter, Majestic Systems

yogurt with its "Save Lids to Save Lives" program. For each specially marked pink yogurt lid mailed in by shoppers, Yoplait donated 50¢ to The Breast Cancer Research Foundation up to a maximum gift of $100,000.

———— • ————

American Express shares the same cause. During the month of October 1998, the company teamed up with the stores that accept their card to help fight breast cancer. For every qualifying purchase made, American Express donated 25¢ to the Komen Foundation up to a maximum donation of $300,000.

———— • ————

The Komen Foundation also benefited from the **California Prune Board's** "Prune the Risk" program, which mixed educational and charitable goals. The Board distributed booklets on preventing breast cancer to consumers (which by the way include eating prunes) and donated a portion of each prune purchase made between October 1998 and April 1999 up to $100,000 to the Foundation.

———— • ————

And to top the list, **Hallmark Gold Crown** stores nationwide supported the same cause with a $1 million donation on Mother's Day 1999. Customers helped make it even larger because a portion of the purchase price of every card purchased between April 18 and May 2 was added to the gift. To encourage support, each customer also got a free greeting card.

———— • ————

For eight years, Maryland-based supermarket chain **Giant Food, Inc.** has sponsored the Apples PLUS program, which has given more than $47 million worth of electronic equipment to over 3,000 elementary and secondary schools in the mid-Atlantic region. The over 150,000 pieces of equipment includes computers, software, printers, televisions, and microscopes.

To qualify for the awards, students and teachers collect dated receipts from Giant Foods. After $30,000 worth of receipts are collected, bundled, and put on deposit with Giant, a school may begin "ordering" equipment. When Giant delivers the goods, they also bring cake for the faculty and ice cream for all the students as a celebration. Smaller prizes are regularly awarded to schools participating in the program.

———————— • ————————

Not one to be outdone, supermarket chain **Farm Fresh** teamed up with Miller Mart and Wachovia Bank to help customers help their local schools with the ABC'S (Audio Visual Equipment, Books and Computers for Schools) program. During the first half of 1999, register tapes from Farm Fresh and their partners turned in at participating schools earned free computers, televisions, software, books, and sporting equipment.

———————— • ————————

The **Target** discount chain created the "School Fundraising Made Simple" program to do just that—make it easy for customers to support the schools of their choice. Select your favorite school and 1% of all purchases made on your Target Guest Card is donated to the qualifying school twice a year. No further effort is necessary on the part of the customer. Target tracks the purchases and makes the donations automatically. So far, the program has generated over $800,000 to more than 50,000 schools.

Nor does Target's largess stop there. In 1998, every pharmacy or health product purchase generated a donation to St. Jude Children's

U.S. companies gave $2.7 billion to higher education in 1996, according to Giving USA: 1997.

Research Hospital in support of its work in finding cures for pediatric cancer and other life-threatening childhood diseases.

———— • ————

Target's zeal runs in the family. Its parent, Minneapolis-based **Dayton Hudson Corp.** makes it a matter of corporate policy to give 5% of profits back to the communities in which they do business. That donation totaled $57 million in 1998.

———— • ————

By year-end 1996, **Pizza Hut's** Book It! program had made reading substantially more palatable for some 22 *million* elementary school students. In schools enrolled in the free program, teachers set monthly reading goals for five months. Every month a child hits the goal, the teacher hands over a gift certificate for a free one-topping Personal Pan Pizza. If everyone in the class meets their goals in four of the five program months, the whole class wins a free pizza party. And, since 10-year-olds probably aren't driving over to Pizza Hut on their own, we bet the chain sold a lot of full-size pies, too.

———— • ————

Companies can also enlist customers in their own favorite philanthropies. **American Express** committed to a $5 million founding sponsorship to the World Monuments Watch, which among other projects is now working to restore the earthquake-damaged St. Francis of Assisi shrine and to erase centuries of pollution damage to the Taj Mahal. The company also offered participants in its Membership Rewards program a piece of the action by allowing the conversion of reward points into cash gifts to the fund *and* matching them dollar for dollar.

———— • ————

If corporate good deeds don't directly involve customers, tell them about it. **Phillips Petroleum Company** used a national advertising campaign to make sure its customers know it takes its environmental responsibilities seriously. One ad highlighted the donation of a former plant site to the Cactus Playa Lake Project, which used it to provide a protected habitat for bald eagles, waterfowl, and other species in the Central Flyway.

A 1997 Cone Communications' survey found that 76% of consumers are likely to change to a brand affiliated with a good cause.

———— ● ————

Water filter maker **Brita Products Company** supports clean water everywhere by acting as a financial sponsor for the annual International Coastal Cleanup program. The one-day effort takes place along beaches and inland shorelines throughout the United States and in 90 countries worldwide. Over 200,000 volunteers participate in the U.S. alone.

———— ● ————

How about combining corporate support of the arts with customer perks? **NationsBank** (now Bank of America) does with regular sponsorships of shows and exhibits in the regions in which it does business. In 1999, the bank helped underwrite the "Art of Glass" exhibition in collaboration with the Contemporary Arts Center of Virginia and the Chrysler Museum of Art. In return, the bank was granted an exclusive showing to which it invited its Professional and Executive Banking clients.

———— ● ————

Reynold Levy managed **AT&T Corporation's** philanthropic efforts for over a decade, during which the nation's largest long-distance company donated over a billion dollars. In his book, *Give and Take*, he cautions charity-minded companies not to think of giving in only financial terms.

Entertaining customers at arts events is a natural, especially in an environment in which the host firm is a valued contributor. Memorable evenings at the opera or theater or dance or symphony can help catalyze and strengthen customer relationships.

—REYNOLD LEVY

"Companies can complement their cash giving with many other resources eagerly sought after by nonprofit organizations," Levy says. "At AT&T, used and state-of-the-art equipment, telecommunications services, advertising, related-cause marketing, promotional and sales gifts, loaned executives, real estate, and use of facilities were all donated in various combinations." Does that generate an idea or two?

———— • ————

Charitable promotions need not be huge affairs. The Keene, New Hampshire–based **Bagel Works** keeps customers coming back to its seven stores by simply asking them to vote for their favorite local charity. The winning charity gets a $500 donation, space in the stores for brochures, product donations, and management assistance.

———— • ————

The West Coast restaurant chain, **Noah's Bagels,** communicates its charitable bent with the "Caring Is Always Kosher" program. The chain asks its customers to help it find worthy causes. Among the results: Unsold bagels are donated to the homeless; new store construction crews are paid to use their skills for community service; and underprivileged children are sent to camp.

———— • ————

In the just-give-us-one-good-reason department: Our local **Ben & Jerry's** ice cream shops promised to donate 50¢ to CDR (Child Development Resources), a nonprofit organization dedicated to helping children and their families, for each sundae they sold in April 1999. Of course, we only went to support CDR.

———— • ————

Your good deeds can also include a sense of fun. Virginia-based car dealer **Oyster Point**

Dodge recently stuck its general manager in a conversion van and hoisted it high with a 50-ton crane . . . for six days. During the stunt, the dealership donated $200 to a local children's hospital for every car sold.

———————— ⬤ ————————

Thrifty Rent-a-Car System, Inc. ran a month-long promotion in September 1998 called "Neighbors Together." For each car rental that month, Thrifty donated at least 50¢ to local charities that specialize in helping children.

———————— ⬤ ————————

Recently, all 75 **Starbucks** locations in and around the Washington, D.C. area gave customers a good reason to stop in for a cup of java. The chain designed covered, reusable coffee cups to support the National Race for the Cure, which benefits breast cancer research and education. Starbucks sold the cups for $6.95 each and threw in a coupon for a free beverage. Then, the chain donated the $2-per-cup profit to the cause.

———————— ⬤ ————————

Consumer product giant **Procter & Gamble** (P&G) combined coupons and philanthropy recently to help terminally ill kids and their families. The company mailed customer coupon packs; and for each coupon redeemed, it donated 10¢ (up to a total of $500,000) to the charitable organization, Give Kids the World.

Another P&G coupon campaign supported the Boomer Esiason Foundation for Cystic Fibrosis. The coupons came with the following message: "For each coupon below you redeem, Procter & Gamble will donate 5¢ (up to $100,000) to the Boomer Esiason Foundation."

———————— ⬤ ————————

Swedish furniture retailer **IKEA** teamed up with two nonprofits to spread the holiday

> Every man's occupation should be beneficial to his fellow man as well as profitable to himself. All else is vanity and folly.
>
> —P. T. Barnum

spirit in 1998. Together with American Forests, it offered customers the "TREEfund Program." Those who bought their fresh-cut Christmas tree, on sale for $20, from IKEA were able to return it on two specified days in January for a $20 IKEA gift certificate. The returned tree was properly mulched and another planted locally to replace it. The furniture and housewares stores also stocked UNICEF greeting cards, the sale of which help fund UNICEF programs for children the world over. And, for every box sold, IKEA donated an extra $1 to the U.S. Committee for UNICEF.

———— ● ————

Teaming up is a great way to leverage your philanthropic might and cross-market your products. Under the auspices of The Better Homes Fund (a nonprofit founded by *Better Homes & Garden's* magazine), direct marketers **Harry and David** and **Jackson & Perkins** donate $5 to KIDSTART, a program that helps homeless preschoolers all across America, for every gift basket of Miracle Roses they sell. The program has yielded $1.6 million for charity since they both began selling the baskets in 1992.

———— ● ————

Event-based programs can drive business and benefit charities. In the dog-eat-dog world of long-distance providers, **10-10-220** differentiated itself from the competition and helped a worthy cause by donating a portion of every call made using the service during the annual Farm-Aid concert.

———— ● ————

Drugstore chain **Eckerd Corporation** teamed up with pharmaceutical giants Johnson & Johnson and McNeil to support the National Safe Kids Campaign. Said the company: "Proceeds from your purchase of Johnson & Johnson or McNeil products at Eckerd will go to support the National Safe Kids Campaign, which provides information on preventing accidental injury in children—the number one killer of children age 14 and under."

———————◉———————

Upscale department store chain **Bloomingdale's** recently brought in customers and raised money for charity at the same time with a one-day "Give a Little, Get a Little Shopping Benefit." Customers bought a $10 ticket in advance. The store added $5 to the $10 from the ticket and donated the entire proceeds to a charity chosen by the customer. The ticket itself was good for a 15% discount at any Bloomingdale's register.

Bloomingdale's also gave its Northern New Jersey customers an invitation to brunch at its Riverside Square store one Sunday morning in March 1999. For $20 per person, customers got a gourmet brunch prepared by a group of area chefs. The chefs, Bloomingdale's, and fine cookware maker Calphalon didn't take a cut, so every penny of customers' $20 contributions went to Share Our Strength (SOS), an organization dedicated to fighting hunger in America. In addition, customers got a free gift and a $20 discount on every $100 worth of Calphalon they bought.

———————◉———————

SOS also attracted help from **Chef's,** catalog retailer of cooking equipment and accessories for the home. The company's catalog includes two pages of specially chosen products from companies such as Calphalon, Wusthof, DeLonghi, and Chef'sChoice. Make a purchase from those pages and a $5 donation is made to SOS-sponsored programs.

———————◉———————

Cooke's Greenhouse recently offered the entire community an added incentive to buy all their spring planting supplies from the privately held small business. Cooke's teamed up with Berkeley Realty Property Management and donated all the profits from selected plants sold during the weekend to the Heritage Humane Society animal shelter.

———— • ————

Another small business, **Ken Matthews Landscape Nursery,** came up with the "Mulch Madness" promotion one March weekend. In addition to "Insane Prices on Mulch," the company sponsored a hoops competition with the proceeds benefiting the Muscular Dystrophy Association. Stop in, shoot two foul shots for $2, and get discounts on products sold at the nursery.

———— • ————

Often, labor is as important as money. The tradition of volunteerism among **Northwestern Mutual Life** recognizes employees with its Employee Community Service Awards program. Each year, the company awards $10,000 to the nonprofit organization represented by its Most Exceptional Volunteer and awards $5,000 each to the charities of 10 Outstanding Volunteers. By the way, Northwestern employees donate 85,000 hours annually to 200 nonprofit organizations.

———— • ————

A subsidiary of Japan's NEC Corporation, Santa Clara, California–based **NEC Electronics Inc.** created the Gifts for Giving program, which makes financial contributions to the charities its employees support with their volunteer efforts. Employees who volunteer at least 25 hours per year earn a grant from the company. And, that means grants to over 100 different nonprofits, including Children's Home of California, American Cancer Society, Ronald McDonald House, and the San Jose Symphony.

———— • ————

United Parcel Service of America, Inc. (UPS) has been helping the underprivileged and building its workforce at the same time, as a founding partner in the Welfare to Work program. Under the program's auspices, UPS hires employees from the nation's welfare rolls—at the same pay and benefits as all other employees in the same jobs. In all, the company has hired over 20,000 former welfare recipients.

In a second program, the world's largest package delivery service sends its managers on one-month paid sabbaticals to work in communities that need help. Since 1968, over 1,000 UPS managers have participated in the UPS Community Internship Program. They have worked for nonprofit agencies mentoring inner-city youth, building temporary housing and schools for migrant farm workers, and so forth. Participants are sent to one of the four internship locations run by nonprofit agencies in Chicago, New York City, Chattanooga, or McAllen, Texas.

———— • ————

Pet supply superchain **PETsMART** created PETsMART Charities, Inc. to drive its charitable activities. As we are writing this, pet food makers Bil-Jac and Pro Plan are donating a penny to the charity for each pound of their own dog and cat food sold at PETsMART during the month. And, Nature's Recipe is donating a $1 for every 17.6-pound bag of their Specific Formula Dog Food or 20-pound bag of their Original Dog or Cat Food sold at the chain.

———— • ————

Mutual fund giant **Fidelity Investments** is keeping customers coming back by helping them manage their charitable giving. The Charitable Gift Fund helps clients contribute to charity and take full advantage of the tax laws at the same time. Donors to the Charitable Gift Fund:

- Receive immediate tax benefits associated with charitable giving
- Avoid capital gains tax on appreciated and restricted securities
- Have the potential to grow over time to increase the charitable gift
- Are assured that Fidelity will see to it that their gift goes to the charity of their choice automatically

———— • ————

Sometimes just providing the opportunity for your customers to do good is all it takes to keep them coming back. **Green Mountain Energy Resources** buys energy from sources that produce it using environmentally sound processes and then resells it over existing utility lines to consumers who are interested in choosing the source of their energy. A Green Mountain customer can order any mix, such as 50% solar, 30% wind, and 20% geothermal energy. They are also given the option of paying bills and receiving newsletters over the Internet instead of using paper and the mails.

———— • ————

Retail eyewear chain **LensCrafters** is a major participant in the "Recycle for Sight" program. Sponsored by the Lions Clubs International, the annual program runs in May and collects used eyeglasses for people in developing countries who normally don't have access to vision correction. The $1 billion chain places collection boxes for old specs in over 700 stores, bringing in scads of old eyewear and, perhaps, people who need new ones.

———————⦿———————

Portland, Oregon's **Hanna** hit a stand-up triple with its "Hannadowns" program, which highlights the quality of its children's clothing, keeps customers coming back, and helps less-fortunate kids all at the same time. Customers are asked to return Hanna clothes to the company after their children have stopped wearing them. In exchange, Hanna offers a 20% discount on their next purchase and donates the returned clothes to needy children. How well does it work? The Hannadowns program receives and redistributes about 10,000 clothing items every month.

———————⦿———————

Steelcase, Inc., subsidiary **Designtex** keeps its environmentally conscious customers coming back by offering competitively priced office fabrics that are 100% biodegradable. In addition, the fabrics are made from organic materials and using nontoxic processes, so they don't harm the environment during their manufacture or use.

———————⦿———————

Wooster, Ohio's **Rubbermaid Inc.** gave customers the first environmentally sound choice with its litter-less lunchbox and was quickly rewarded with about 10% of the entire lunchbox market. Inspired by a Canadian program that required a litter-free lunch once each week, in the early 1990s, the product generated widespread publicity and heavy demand.

———————⦿———————

From the it-speaks-for-itself department: UK-based drug giant **SmithKline Beecham PLC** formed a $1 billion partnership with the

World Health Organization in 1998. For its part, the company will donate the drugs needed to eliminate Lymphatic Filariasis, one of the world's six eradicable diseases and one that is currently afflicting approximately 120 million people around the world.

———— • ————

Tom's of Maine built its toothpaste brand on all-natural ingredients and "earth-friendly packaging." Tom's, which celebrated its 25th birthday in 1998, also donates 10% of its annual profits to environmental causes.

———— • ————

As Lexington, Massachusetts–based footwear maker **The Stride Rite Corporation** tells its customers: "There are moments when the choices you make count a little more." This is especially true of the line of kids' shoes featuring the Save the Children Federation's logo created by the company. Each time customers buy a pair of the logo shoes, Stride Rite makes a donation of 3% to 4% of the retail price to Save the Children. This program runs from August 1, 1997 through December 1, 1999 and the company guarantees a donation of at least $82,500.

———— • ————

Each year on cardholders' anniversaries, **Discover** sends off its promised "Cashback Bonus" checks, which amounts to something between .25% and 1% of annual purchases, depending on a published formula. The accompanying cover letter thanks card members for their loyalty and includes endorsement instructions and a pre-addressed envelope just in case they want to donate their checks to the Make-a-Wish Foundation. It seems that quite a few have: Since 1988, Discover cardholders have given $1.3 *billion* to the charity in returned checks and personal contributions.

———— ◆ ————

Ukrop's also offers a shopping cart full of philanthropic programs. Under the auspices of the Golden Gift Program, the grocer tracks total household spending at the store via the Valued Customer card. Then, a mass-customized newsletter is sent to customers with their family's purchase total included in the form of a "Golden Certificate." Customers give their favorite charity the Golden Certificate, which is returned to Ukrop's for a corresponding slice of the chain's $675,000 donation pie. In 1998, 118 groups received over $1,000 each, while the balance of the donation pool was split among hundreds of other nonprofits. Overall, the program has donated over $7.4 million since 1987.

Ukrop's also reaches out to its vendors to create charitable programs. Two recent local examples:

- General Mills agreed to donate 5¢ each on a group of select products sold at Ukrop's to St. Joseph's Villa's Helping Hands campaign, a program assisting needy children and their families.
- Ray-O-Vac agreed to donate one battery for each one sold at Ukrop's to benefit the Broomfield Learning Center, a provider of education to some of the area's less fortunate kids.

———— ◆ ————

Help can also have an individual focus, as demonstrated by this story involving corporate travel agency **Rosenbluth International:** During an off-site sales meeting in North Dakota, employees met a woman who needed a double lung transplant to survive. On a waiting list without much hope, the woman's plight moved them to find a way to help. In a company-wide effort, they found the answer in Memphis, flew the woman and her family in, and stuck around as support. The operation was successful.

Remembers CEO Hal Rosenbluth in his book, *Good Business:* "It's not every day we can help save a life, but we can make the lives we touch better, and that's an amazing way to do business."

———— • ————

Santa Rosa, California–based **Rella Good Cheese Co.** targeted sales of $4 million in 1998 and expected profits of $10,000 to $20,000. The company decided early in the fiscal year that it would donate all those pre-tax profits to charity.

———— • ————

And there's actor Paul Newman's **Newman's Own** food products company. We'll let the company say it: "Paul Newman donates all profits, after taxes, from the sale of these products for educational and charitable purposes." In fact, Newman's Own has donated over $90 million to charities to date; and the count rises every time another jar of spaghetti sauce, bottle of salad dressing, or package of popcorn gets scanned at the cash registers of the nation's markets.

6

REWARD
EVERY
CUSTOMER

ere's an exercise that might help you understand why every customer deserves reward. Run a list of a dozen of your biggest customers this month, or quarter, or year, and try to track down that customer's first contact with your company.

If you are anything like us, you will find that very few of those great customers walked in the door with a bang. At our company, they usually called looking for one book they were having a problem finding. A lot of them didn't call with an order at all. They wanted to comment on something we had written or to ask for information, and they were surprised to find out we sold books.

That led us to an important lesson: Every person who calls in a small order and everyone who makes a casual request for information has the potential to become a great customer. So, why not treat them that way from the start?

All customers deserve reward from the moment they contact your company. It doesn't have to be a huge reward, but it does need to make them feel that you honestly value the fact that they chose to contact your company.

Let's start with the simplest, least expensive reward there is:

TELL THEM YOU CARE

Sam Walton was the driving force in the creation of **Wal-Mart Stores, Inc.** He knew darn well what customers meant to his company and he made sure employees did, too. One way is reflected in the Wal-Mart stores' employee pledge: "I solemnly promise and declare that for every customer that comes within ten feet of me, I will smile, look them in the eye, and greet them, so help me Sam."

In a world where it is not unusual to walk into a store, do your shopping, and make a purchase without a single store employee bothering to speak to you, the simple things go a long way. We know a loyal customer of **Berkeley Cleaners** who was pleased as punch that the counterperson remembered his name each and every time after his initial visit.

Salespeople at Denver, Colorado–based menswear store **Grassfield's** also make it a point to remember customers by name, a habit that automatically takes the relationship to a more personal level.

Being polite doesn't mean "yessing" customers to death. Sometimes, they need some knowledgeable advice, *tactfully* delivered. "If you really are the expert, don't be afraid to say 'no' to the customer when saying 'no' is to their benefit," says T. Scott Gross in his book, **Outrageous!** "Unlike all the other companies that will do anything just to make the sale, you are doing the right thing to make a customer."

Phone reps at business-to-business cataloger **New Pig Corporation** are just waiting for a rea-

> If you remember my name, you pay me a subtle compliment; you indicate that I have made an impression on you. Remember my name and you add to my feeling of importance.
>
> —DALE CARNEGIE

son to drop you a line. The company keeps a selection of assorted greeting cards on a shelf in their order department. When a customer mentions a birthday or other noteworthy occurrence, the reps simply reach for a card to commemorate the event, fill it out on the spot, and out it goes in that day's mail.

————— ● —————

Just say thank you! It is amazing how often we do business with companies and never hear those simple words. Get your car serviced at Statesville, North Carolina–based **Hendrick's Honda,** and within a couple of days, a card arrives in your mailbox thanking you for trusting Hendrick's to work on your car. No big deal, but maybe just enough to steer you toward that dealership when it's time for another service call or the newest model.

————— ● —————

The final day of a luxury vacation voyage on **Crystal Cruise's** Symphony ship is a bittersweet experience. Well, in this case, more sweet than bitter: As passengers readied for departure at the end of a recent Scandinavian cruise, they found a handwritten note in their cabins along with a box of Norwegian chocolates. The gifts were from the cabin maids, known as stewardesses, who offered the chocolates as a reminder of the time aboard the ship.

————— ● —————

On the 40th anniversary of its card, **American Express** sent cardholders a personalized letter of thanks and a small gift: a phone message pad. Each time members use it, they are reminded that American Express sent an unsolicited, no obligation, no-strings-attached message of thanks. Nice.

————— ● —————

> The sale merely consummates the courtship. Then the marriage begins. How good the marriage is depends on how well the relationship is managed by the seller.
>
> —THEODORE LEVITT

When was the last time you got a note from your hairdresser? Virginia-based **Fitzgerald's** beauty salons send a thank-you card to first-time customers, which reminds them of the their hairdresser's name and invites them to phone with any questions and concerns about their hair.

———————⦿———————

How about your exterminator? **Terminex,** the Nationwide Pest Control Experts, lets its customers know it appreciates the opportunity to wipe out their pests. After a Terminex appointment, customers get a thank you in the mail that includes a business card.

———————⦿———————

We aren't real estate moguls by any means, but we do think of local **NationsBanc Mortgage Corporation** account executive Kim Tahey as "our" mortgage banker. Kim is the first loan maker we've ever regularly heard from after the loan closed. One of her techniques: "Happy Thanksgiving" cards (last time with a coupon booklet for free items at the local Manhattan Bagel restaurant) to thank customers for their business.

———————⦿———————

Cataloger **Norm Thompson** says thanks. Each order arrives with a thank-you card to its customers, letting them know their business is appreciated and expressing the hope that their customers call on them again soon.

———————⦿———————

Orders from **Frontgate's** catalog also generate a thank-you letter with a little extra. The letter reiterates their extended return policy (see Chapter 5) and includes a 15% discount certificate.

———————⦿———————

Inc. magazine clued us in on this creative thank-you idea from Omaha, Nebraska–based consulting firm **Bass & Associates,** whose 75 employees are usually working in customer's locations around the country. Every month, founder Deborah Bass sends these employees a batch of brownies to share with their customers—a tasteful way of saying thanks.

———— • ————

Why bother with a single customer? **Southwest Airlines** conducted a study in 1995 that found its flights did not break the profitability barrier until the 76th passenger. More importantly, writes executive vice president Colleen Barrett in *Customer Service,* "only 5 passengers per flight—or 3 million of the 40 million passengers Southwest carried that year—accounted for the line's total annual profit of over $179.3 million. So losing just one passenger per flight because of bad service would reduce our profits by 20%."

———— • ————

Make sure employees know how much a single customer is worth. In *1,001 Ways to Inspire,* Frank Meeks, the owner of a chain of **Domino's Pizza** stores, explains how he adds it up for his staff: "Our customers do business with us at least once a week, spending close to $500 annually, not including your tips," Meeks tells them. "That's $2,500 over 5 years, which is what it costs us if they leave us because they are unhappy. And the unhappy customer tells about a dozen people about their negative experience, multiplying the damage even further."

———— • ————

Ford Motor Company combined a thank you and a coupon to encourage their customers to once again put themselves behind the wheel of the station wagon of the '90s, a new sports utility vehicle. Explorer owners were mailed a "Loyalty Bonus" worth $500 off the purchase

It's easy to take regular and walk-in customers for granted. Don't. Thank them for choosing to do business with you.

—RON ZEMKE AND KRISTIN ANDERSON IN *DELIVERING KNOCK-YOUR-SOCKS-OFF SERVICE* or lease price of its 1998 and 1999 Explorer and Expedition models.

───────●───────

Ford's luxury **Lincoln** line also uses the technique. They call it "Special Appreciation Cash." Current Lincoln Town Car owners, who bought their 1986–1998 cars new and still own them, are given $1,000 cashback on the purchase or Red Carpet Lease of a new Town Car. By the way, this is the car that ranked #1 in owner loyalty in a 1997 Polk Company survey of high-income households.

───────●───────

General Motors certainly isn't going to let the competition do all the loyalty appreciating. In 1998, its Buick division offered some strong incentives to customers, including 0.98% financing and no payments for 98 days. It also issued *"Loyalty First"* certificates worth up to $1,000 to Buick owners who purchased new cars in the 1986 through 1998 model years.

───────●───────

The easiest business you can earn is the business referred to you by satisfied customers. Referral rewards make good sense since they encourage future recommendations and build customer loyalty at the same time. **Diamond Springs Water,** in Richmond, Virginia, thanks its customers who refer new customers with two free 5-gallon bottles of water.

───────●───────

When **Merry Maids** customers recommend a new prospect who signs up, the cleaning franchise rewards them with a $20 deduction on their next scheduled cleaning.

It's also nice to have an anniversary you don't have to feel guilty about forgetting. On the one-year anniversary of a customer's association with the company, Merry Maids sur-

A Yankelovich Partners' survey asked 2,500 shoppers what "was most important to you regarding customer service." Courtesy, knowledgeability, and friendliness were the top answers. Almost 66% felt salespeople did not care about them or their needs.

prised them with a vase of fresh flowers, along with a handwritten thank you for past loyalty and future business.

———————●———————

Seattle, Washington–based **Cruise Specialists** created the 1999 Sea Treasures Referral Program to build referrals from its existing customers. The company sent customers referral cards on which they write their own names and distribute to potential passengers. If the new customer books a cruise, the referrer gets a free gift and an entry into a drawing for a $1,000 Future Cruise Credit.

———————●———————

In 1997, **AT&T** decided to stop sending checks to competitor's customers and instead thank its own customers. The company sent out "loyalty" packages to its 20 million customers. They contained something AT&T knew their customers could use—free long distance minutes. The thank you back: 600,000 signups for additional services, according to *The Journal of Business Strategy*.

———————●———————

Big-ticket buys should generate a correspondingly valuable thank you. When San Francisco realtor **McGuire** connects its customers to high-value properties, it thanks them with a splendid leather gift folder embossed with the company name. Inside is a $500 gift certificate for San Francisco's own Gump's department store, a purveyor of "the rare, the unique, the imaginative since 1861."

———————●———————

Thanks can come in many forms. How about a special event to reward special customers? Japan's **Oura Oil** treated members of its "Five-Up Club" to a visit to a local orchard where they could pick their own fruit. The event drew over 300 customers.

> **We want customers to hear the smile in our agents' voices, which means we have to create a work environment where employees really do smile.**
>
> —**VOICE SERVICES FOR SPRINT'S LORI LOCKHART** IN *TRAINING*

————— • —————

Or how about the opportunity to get into a special event? **Continental Airlines** recently reserved blocks of tickets at New York City's Carnegie Hall for its OnePass members. On two nights in June 1998, members got an inside line on seats to an award-winning show featuring the music of Judy Garland, staged by Lorna Luft (Garland's daughter) and an all-star cast including Robert Goulet, Alan King, and Vicki Carr.

————— • —————

New York City–based **American International Group's** (AIG) Risk Management Group writes commercial insurance for businesses where the premiums alone run into millions of dollars. It thanks its customers and builds relationships at the same time with a bevy of special events year-round. As owners of the famous New England ski resort, Stow, AIG entertains clients on the slopes. It also sponsors a VIP tent for its guests at the U.S. Open at Forest Hills and regular golf outings at Westchester's Mor Far course, which the company also owns. Other AIG-sponsored events clients have enjoyed are a mystery dinner followed by an AIG product fair and, one of the favorites, a fishing excursion on a charter followed by lunch on land at a nearby restaurant.

ASK FOR THEIR NAMES

You can't reward them if you don't know who they are. **WestPoint Stevens' Bed, Bath & Linen Factory Outlets** reach out to people with their coupons. To take advantage of one of their 10% off coupons (readily available in area publications as well as in fliers inside the stores), you must fill out the name and address infor-

Only if you really know the people who use your products can you win a place, respectfully and affectionately, in their lives.

—Charlotte Beers,
former chairman of
Ogilvy & Mather in
Leader to Leader

mation on the coupon itself. The outlet shop has created a mailing list from those names and regularly sends out "Preferred Customer Coupons" to attract repeat sales.

———————— • ————————

Madison, New Jersey–based **Schering-Plough Corporation** makes the world's leading prescription antihistamine, but it knows that since most allergies are suffered seasonally, users of Claritin may not have had a prescription filled in nine months or more. When spring comes again, so does a full-blown Claritin ad campaign featuring a toll-free number to call to receive a $5 rebate certificate for purchases of Claritin. The rebate collects customer contact information and a short survey of symptoms, and each rebate check is sent to the customer with *another* rebate certificate for the next purchase.

———————— • ————————

Grassfield's, a Denver, Colorado–based men's store, well understands the role spouses play in their success. So, the store asks for the names of its customers' spouses and keeps them in the loop by sending specific mailings on special dates, such as Father's Day and birthdays. Grassfield's even suggests appropriate gifts based on the customer's history and past purchases.

———————— • ————————

One of the reasons the Atlanta-based **Ritz-Carlton** so often pleasantly surprises its guests is that the hotel chain's employees pursue information with *quiet* determination. A paragon of service, the $1 billion company asks frequent guests to complete a questionnaire of preferences. The survey is used to enhance the guest's future stays with personally picked items, such as a fruit plate, complimentary

Personal Information Is Privileged Information

If you plan to ask customers to divulge personal information, be prepared to explain your policy for its use and protection. Here at **The Business Reader,** we make it a strict rule never to sell or barter our customers' names, contact or sales information. Further, in an era when everyone knows that customer data is money, it makes good sense to offer something in return, such as a free newsletter subscription or discount . . . on the spot.

A Harris survey found that eight of every ten U.S. adults feel they have no control over how companies collect and use their personal information.

There is only one valid definition of business purpose: to create a customer.

—PETER DRUCKER

shoe travel bags, or a favorite magazine or newspaper. After that, as employees learn more about customers, they unobtrusively enter the info into the chain's customer database. Eventually, all the customers know is that no other hotel chain does for them what the Ritz-Carlton does.

MAKE THE NEXT SALE

One sale leads to another. Or, it better, if you plan to build your business. Drug maker **Merck & Co.** well knows that lesson. When customers buy a package of its new, and expensive, Pepcid AC acid reducer, it comes with an offer to get more of the product free. Buy four packages and send in their UPC symbols with register receipts, and back comes a free box containing 18 doses.

————— ● —————

A gift certificate is how many new customers are introduced to Ohio-based **Mario's International Aurora Hotel & Spa.** To keep them coming back for more, during checkout, the spa invites them to purchase future gift certificates, valid for themselves or anyone else they choose, at a 20% discount from regular prices.

————— ● —————

Silicon Valley's **Symantec Corporation,** makers of highly respected Norton anti-virus software, uses a two-tier rebate program to build business and repeat business. Recently, it offered a $20 rebate on products such as Anti-Virus, First Aid, and VirusScan. The rebate check arrives with a thank-you "Gift Check" and another rebate offer—this time for a $10 rebate on additional Symantec products.

————— ● —————

The order takers at leading book wholesaler **Ingram Book Company** start making the next sale before they hang up on the last. Customer reps who take telephone orders from the company's bookstore and library customers are armed with a short list of recommended titles each week. Place an order that includes a group of business books, and you are sure to get politely asked if you would like to hear about this week's business pick.

------------●------------

Discover Card uses its cardholders' calls to customer service as an opportunity to build its business. After your business is complete, you might hear something like this: "Before you hang up, do you have any high interest rate credit card balances you would like to transfer to Discover?" Say yes and it's a case of "Let it be so." Just give the rep the name of the credit card issuer, the amount due, and the due date, and Discover takes care of the rest.

------------●------------

Here's an idea that is elegantly circular: Concord, New Hampshire's **Bible Bookstore** trades gift certificates in return for the privilege of displaying its titles to potential customers attending church events. The churches use the gift certificates as raffle and door prizes. And, the winners go to the Bible Bookstore to spend them.

------------●------------

Your repeat discount doesn't have to be open-ended. If you bought women's clothing at the **Liz Claiborne** outlet stores in the spring of 1998, you received a 25% Spring Fashion Bonus good on any specially ticketed sale item. The repeat business hook: the coupon was stamped with the current date and was valid for only 30 days after the initial sale.

We couldn't confirm this story, but because it makes such a good point about knowing your customer, we had to share it: A plainly dressed couple asked to see the president of Harvard University. After a long wait—they didn't look very important—they told him they wanted to create a memorial for their son, who had died after spending one year at the school.

The president quickly declined. Harvard couldn't have statues all over the grounds. How about a building? Looking over the unimpressive pair, the president suggested that they couldn't possibly afford a building. Harvard, he told them, had over $7.5 *million* in facilities.

On hearing the amount, the woman turned to her husband and said that perhaps a whole university would be a better tribute to their son. And so, Mr. and Mrs. Leland Stanford left Harvard and financed and built California's Stanford University.

Think it's too expensive to convince an existing customer to buy again? Listen to Tom Petzinger, Jr., *Wall Street Journal* columnist and author of *The New Pioneers* (Simon & Schuster, 1999): "In many cases the cost of acquiring a customer began to exceed the cost of the product itself—roughly $50 in the case of the average direct-mail customer, for instance."

———— ● ————

Eddie Bauer's outlet store chain encourages repeat business with a similar program. Customers get a point of sale coupon for a 10% discount on anything in the store for the next 30 days.

———— ● ————

Place your first order with direct marketer **Reliable Office Products,** and the company sends you more than just office supplies. First-time buyers receive a certificate valid for a 10% discount off their next order.

———— ● ————

Fort Worth, Texas–based home furniture and accessories retailer **The Bombay Company, Inc.** doesn't wait for customers to finish their first purchase to sign them up for more. The store offers a 10% discount on that initial purchase in return for opening an in-store charge account. The account triggers regular mailings of the Bombay catalog and special sales offers.

The chain does not stop there. It tracks the credit card's usage and if it is not used regularly, a postcard with a 10% discount offer soon arrives:

"It's been awhile since we've seen you at Bombay. Come in and see what's new in the way of furniture collections, wall décor, home accents and more! Plus, bring this card and be amazed at the savings you'll enjoy as a preferred credit card customer."

———— ● ————

If you want your customers to come back, tell 'em so. New York City–based **J. Crew Group, Inc.'s** catalog division keeps track of whether or not its customers are placing orders; and if not, they send a catalog with this message on the cover, "You've been missed here at J. Crew." As a way to get reacquainted, the company also offers a $20 credit on orders of at least $80.

––––––––– ◉ –––––––––

Eddie Bauer misses you, too. Recently, the direct marketer sent a catalog to shoppers who haven't ordered lately that offered the opportunity to "Rediscover Eddie Bauer." To help shoppers decide to buy again, Eddie Bauer offered free delivery and free returns to those who ordered at least $100 from the catalog.

––––––––– ◉ –––––––––

And, so does **The Company Store,** a direct marketer of down, feather, and other natural products for the home. Lapsed customers get a personalized letter and a "$20 Welcome Back Bond" good for $20 off their next order of $125 or more.

––––––––– ◉ –––––––––

The **Quality Paperback Book Club** (QPB) sends customers who haven't ordered lately a greeting card with the sentiment: "It's the pits without you. Please come back!" To entice you to do just that, QPB offers four books for $4, plus shipping and handling.

QPB also uses a postcard from the vice president of Customer Service to get customers busy buying. In this case, customers may take 50% off any books in the latest QPB Review just by listing the titles and item numbers directly on the card and mailing it back by a certain date.

––––––––– ◉ –––––––––

New York City's **Crunch Fitness** goes after inactive customers *before* their membership commitments are over with its "AWOL" clinics. The clinics are run by exercise counselors, who provide tips and instruction combined with motivational advice, giving members good reasons to restart their workouts and reenlist when the time comes.

If you're not serving the customer, your job is to be serving someone who is.

—Jan Carlzon, CEO of Scandinavian Airlines

Saks Holdings, Inc.'s Saks Fifth Avenue chain used an upgrade to its in-store credit card system as an opportunity to suggest that inactive account holders "rediscover the privileges of your Saks Fifth Avenue credit card." The incentive for returning was a 10% savings on nearly all merchandise in the store for an entire day's shopping spree of the cardholder's choice between March 7 and May 31, 1999.

In the movie theater business, you are only as good as the films you run. But the Knoxville, Tennessee–based **Regal Cinemas, Inc.** chain makes a good play for repeat business with its Gift Ticket Books, which they bill as "Santa's Favorite Stocking Stuffer." The certificates in the books are good for movie admissions as well as for refreshments at the concession stand. More importantly, they get customers asking, "What's playing at *Regal?*"

In a drive to build its share of its customers' air shipments, **United Parcel Service** (UPS) recently sent out an offer that was tough to refuse. Try the service for at least one package and fill out a short survey, and in return, get a coupon book good for $40 in savings on UPS air services.

Here's a neat way to create the next sale: Tell your customer how to put your products to other uses. The classic example is **Church & Dwight Company's** Arm & Hammer baking soda. It takes a lot of baking to use a box of baking soda, but as a deodorizer in the fridge it doesn't last nearly as long.

The Procter & Gamble Company (P&G), the world's largest household products maker, is

Why haven't they come back? A Harvard Business Review *study found that* two-thirds *of customers stop doing business with companies because they feel unappreciated, neglected, or treated indifferently.*

trying the same technique with its Bounce fabric softener sheets. The product was designed to be used in dryers, but the company wasn't happy about having Bounce's sales restricted to dryer loads. So, P&G created a series of ads showing consumers how to use Bounce in other ways. Among the suggestions: use them as fresheners in drawers, blanket chests, gym bags, and even sneakers.

——————— ● ———————

Copier king **Xerox Corporation** keeps customers returning for their replacement toner cartridges by making them members in the Xerox Green Team. It couldn't be any easier: Every toner cartridge comes with a postage-paid label and reusable packaging that customers can use to mail the old toner cartridge back to the company. The cartridge gets refurbished instead of discarded, and the customer gets a $5 check good toward the purchase of their next toner cartridge.

——————— ● ———————

The **Busch Gardens** theme park wants you back . . . tomorrow. When visitors leave the park at the end of the day, they are automatically offered an $11 admission to return the next day. That's a pretty hefty discount off the $30+ daily ticket price.

. . . AND THE NEXT SALE, AND THE NEXT

Frequent customer clubs are a common way to build repeat business. There are enough coffee bars in our small town to keep most of the state revved up, so **The Coffeehouse** makes its bid for repeat business with its Coffee Club Membership Card. Each time the customer buys a pound or half a pound of coffee, their card is so marked and the 13th pound is free.

> A salesman is one who sells goods that won't come back to customers who will.
>
> —UNKNOWN SOURCE

In an era of relationship marketing, sales excellence is demonstrated by the number of customers who make a second purchase.

—Louis Boone
AUTHOR, *Quotable Business*

———— ● ————

Local competitor **Williamsburg Coffee & Tea** has its own club card, which pays off with a free pound of coffee after 10 pounds are purchased. We like another perk for coffee lovers, the free cup of freshly brewed coffee (which incidentally allows the client to try any number of new flavors and come back for those).

———— ● ————

The rewards don't have to be more of the same. **ConAgra Frozen Foods'** Healthy Choice purchases air miles from the major airlines to fuel its frequent buyer program. It offers customers 500 frequent flyer miles for every 10 Healthy Choice products they purchase. Customers have until year-end 1999 to request their miles, which are mailed to directly to them, and then must be sent to one of the participating airlines for deposit to their air mile accounts.

———— ● ————

Credit cards are a common frequent buyer vehicle: **The TJX Companies, Inc.'s** discount chains tie their frequent buyer programs to the TJX Visa Card. The card gives buyers a 5% bonus on T.J. Maxx and Marshalls purchases, and a 1% bonus every time they use the card elsewhere. Reward certificates are sent automatically to cardholders each time they reach $15. In turn, the certificates can be used toward any purchase at T.J. Maxx or Marshalls stores.

———— ● ————

L. L. Bean, Inc.'s Outdoor Advantage program is tied to a Platinum Plus Visa credit card that offers credit limits up to $100,000. Sign up and get free FedEx shipping on orders, free monogramming, and savings coupons with each purchase. For every $200 spent with the company, members receive a $6 coupon; and for every $200 spent elsewhere, a $1 coupon—redeemable at L. L. Bean, of course.

————— • —————

The Sharper Image also uses a credit card to power its frequent buyer program. The first purchase on the company's VISA earns a $10 gift certificate, and then every $2,000 charged on the card earns a $25 certificate.

————— • —————

BMG Music Service combined music and its own VISA card to create its frequent buyer program. Sign up for the no-fee card and earn three points for every dollar spent at BMG and one point for all other purchases. Points are redeemable toward tickets to concerts, stereo equipment, and BMG music catalog CDs and merchandise.

————— • —————

Musicland Stores Corporation makes sure customers get the most play from its Replay frequent buyer program by making purchases in both the Sam Goody and On Cue chains eligible. For a small fee, customers get a 15% discount on signup day and then, earn points redeemable for store merchandise. It also sends its more than 520,000 members a regular newsletter.

————— • —————

Borders Group, Inc.'s Waldenbooks chain designed a similar program under the name "Preferred Reader." Customers pay a $10 fee to sign up and, in return, receive a 10% discount on all their book buys, plus points that are transformed automatically into store certificates.

————— • —————

Padow's Hams & Deli gives its customers two reasons to keep coming back. They offer two different "Free Sandwich Club Cards,"

> Companies spend 6 to 10 times more to acquire new customers than they do to retain existing customers. But a 5% increase in customer retention can have a bottom-line profit increase of 75%, depending on the industry.
>
> —DON NEAL, DIRECTOR OF BUSINESS DEVELOPMENT FOR HALLMARK BUSINESS EXPRESSIONS

> "Loyalty" means you retain a customer and increase the business you do with that customer, developing a relationship so this customer will not be lured away to the competition with the promise of a lower price.
>
> —LISA FORD IN
> BEST PRACTICES IN
> CUSTOMER SERVICE

depending on their customers' appetites. One card is valid for regular sandwiches valued at $2.95 to $4.50. The other is for their elite "Mile High Sandwiches," which cost a hefty $8.50 each. Both cards offer the customer's 9th sandwich free.

———————

Stamford, Connecticut restaurant **David's American Food & Drink** created a database of their best customers and mailed them an invitation to join "David's Regulars." The frequent diner club starts by giving customers their choice of a 15% discount, a free bottle of wine, or a free appetizer on their first visit as members. After that initial offer, "David's Regulars" use their membership card to earn a free entrée on their tenth visit.

———————

The Veranda Restaurant at **Fort Magruder Inn** created "Brunch, Lunch & Dinner" cards to drive repeat business. Each card works the same way but may be used by only one person for only one specific type of meal. For example, after customer comes in for lunch five times, the sixth lunch is free.

———————

Cracker Barrel Old Country Stores like feeding you, so it created a frequent diner program called the "Neighbor Reward." Each visit to the restaurant chain earns points toward gift certificates worth $10 each. And, the chain uses the program to distribute a newsletter and reward statement to each member.

———————

Illusions Unlimited, an Ohio-based chain of full-service salons, keep customers coming back with its "VIP Program." The salon punches the VIP card for each haircut, entitling the customer to their seventh cut free. For those who would only stop in on special occasions, there is a catch: The card must be punched at least once every six weeks or it becomes invalid.

———— ◈ ————

The Helpful Hardware Club is **Ace Hardware Corporation's** frequent buyer program. Free to all customers, the membership card–based club gives 10 points redeemable for gift certificates for each dollar spent. Ace also includes plenty of soft benefits for customers of its 5,000-store hardware cooperative. There is a special club rep in each store to assist members, an exclusive area on the company's Web site, a free newsletter, and special sales offers.

———— ◈ ————

Direct marketer **Eddie Bauer** created a points-based reward system to keep its customers coming back. Members of Eddie Bauer's Rewards get 10 points for every dollar spent in the catalog and a bonus of five points for every dollar spent when they use Eddie Bauer's own credit card. Amass 5,000 points and along comes a $10 gift certificate.

———— ◈ ————

Used and rare book dealer **The Book House** keeps it very simple. The store encourages repeat business with its "Regular Customer Card." Customers earn $10 in free books for every $100 spent.

———— ◈ ————

Wait'll they get their Hanes on you. **Sara Lee Corporation** has its fingers in a lot of pies, about $20 billion worth annually. It is the leading U.S. maker of intimate apparel, underwear, and socks, and owns brands such as L'eggs, Hanes, Bali, Playtex, and Champion. So, when you get your L'eggs Frequent Buyer Club card, it works at the factory outlets for all

Three Frequency Program Warnings

1. Don't start something you can't finish: Pepsico offered a Harrier military jet (that your average Joe isn't allowed to own) to customers who collected enough redemption points. One did . . . and sued.

2. Don't assume the difficult is impossible: The Chart House restaurant chain offered a free trip around the world for two to customers who ate in all 65 locations worldwide . . . 41 did and collected 82 free trips.

3. Don't give away something that isn't yours: Remember that when US Air gives away a roundtrip ticket, it doesn't cost them what it would cost you to give away the same ticket (unless you have an airline of your own).

Do you believe the old adage, "The customer is always right"? I don't—never have and never will. I do, however believe "The customer is always the customer, and I want that customer to always be mine."

—JOHN HARTLEY, PROMUS HOTEL CORP., IN *BEST PRACTICES IN CUSTOMER SERVICE*

those brands. One stamp is received for every $10 spent in any combination of the above stores. Ten stamps earn a 15% discount, and 15 stamps earn a 20% discount.

Hecht's department store chain also wants to get their hands on you. To help encourage return visits, Hecht's offers customers free membership in their Hosiery Club. Customers get one free pair of hose for every 12 pairs purchased, and the store gets to tempt them with all its other goodies each time they visit.

Casual Corner, retailer of moderately priced sportswear and business attire geared toward working women, wants to get their hands on you even more. It offers its customers the "Hosiery Club Card." Buy six pairs of pantyhose and get the seventh pair free, whether you buy them one at a time or in one mad fling.

Just For Feet, which bills itself as the "World's Largest Athletic Shoe Store," gives sneaker buyers a reason to be loyal with its frequent buyer plan. Simply put, "the 13th pair is always free." Sound like a lot of sneakers to you? No kids, right?

Frequent customer programs are spreading fast in cyberspace. **America Online** (AOL) customers can reduce their monthly fees by earning points in the AOL Reward program. Points accumulate for making purchases at participating vendors or completing AOL opinion and feedback surveys. Recently, three online stock brokerages offered AOL Reward points to members who opened online accounts with them. Among them was E-Trade, which offered new clients 13,200 points or enough to pay their AOL subscription for six months.

———— • ————

Registered visitors to **CBS SportsLine** Web site earn points and sweepstakes entries for simply looking over the site. Each page viewed gets an automatic entry in a drawing for a $1 million prize and also racks up points for the visitor. Points may be redeemed on the Web site for merchandise and special events including private celebrity chats.

———— • ————

Sign up and shop through the **Netcentives, Inc.'s** ClickRewards Web site, and all your purchases earn ClickMiles, redeemable with American Airlines for free flights. Membership in ClickRewards is free; the merchants linked to the site pay the company, so you don't have to.

———— • ————

We are fans of **PETsMART** even though we don't currently have pets. They know how to keep customers coming back. Get your free membership cards in the superstore's Grooming Club and after eight visits, get a complimentary groom or bath service. As an added incentive to participate, PETsMART gave two punches instead of one for groom or bath services purchased during March 1999.

———— • ————

Retailers who set up shop in Newport News, Virginia's **Patrick Henry Mall** also get the benefits of the facility's Mall X-Tras preferred customer program. Get a free membership card and purchases made in mall stores earn points that are redeemable for gift certificates for merchandise from the mall's stores.

———— • ————

Harrah's Entertainment, Inc. created the Total Gold Program for its loyal gamblers.

How do you keep 'em coming back online? A survey of the 100 most successful online retailers by International Data Corporation found that 92% use structured loyalty programs to promote repeat sales.

Companies have dis-
covered that the
longer that customers
stay with a company,
the more profitable
they are.

—Philip Kotler in
Kotler on Marketing

Points are earned for dollars played at the slots as well as the gaming tables, no matter if you win or lose. When 200 points accumulate, players can redeem them at an in-house ATM for "Total Reward" vouchers at a rate of $1 for 40 points. The vouchers are good toward food, the hotel bill, Harrah's shows and vacations, or just in case they've gone bust, cash.

———————— • ————————

Go ahead, talk! **New Zealand Telecom** established the Talking Points program to reward frequent callers. Points are earned based on the amount of your monthly bill and can be traded for free long-distance calls, movie passes, specialty services such as call waiting, phone cards, and even faxes, cell phones, and pagers.

———————— • ————————

Buy a computer printer from **College & University Computers** (CUC) and it comes with the "Buyer's Club Card for Printers." It entitles customers to a lifetime discount of 10% off new printer cartridges. This simple program goes a long way toward helping CUC capture what is often the most lucrative part of an equipment sale—the ongoing need to replace regularly consumed parts.

———————— • ————————

And, what gets more regularly consumed than batteries? Fort Worth, Texas–based **Tandy Corporation** created a free PowerZone Card for the customers of its almost 7,000 RadioShack stores. Those who use their card to stock up on batteries at RadioShack save on each purchase: 10% off on one pack, 20% off on two packs, and 30% off on three packs or more. By making purchases with the PowerZone Card, customers may also receive up to $23 in free batteries.

Sears, Roebuck and Company entices its Canadian customers to keep spending with its credit card–based Sears Club. Customers join free and every dollar subsequently spent earns a point. Points convert to gift certificates or air miles.

Choice Hotels International Inc.'s properties include more than 2,200 Comfort, Clarion, Quality, and Sleep Inns, and its Guest Privileges program spans all four chains. The plan gives members 10 points for each dollar they spend in any of the hotels, and the points are redeemable for free room nights. Members also get benefits such as late checkouts and room upgrades when available.

Weehawken, New Jersey–based **Hanover Direct, Inc.'s** Kitchen & Home catalog unit created a fee-based Buyer's Club. In return for the $25 annual fee, shoppers get immediate savings of 10% on every item in their catalog and an exclusive toll-free hotline for priority ordering and customer service. If customers are not satisfied with the program, the $25 fee is refundable within the first 30 days.

Provide for your healthy lifestyle at **The Health Shelf,** a single location retailer that sells natural health and food products, and for $10 a year you can buy Preferred Customer status. The program offers exclusive specials, but the main draw is a 21% discount on all purchases made on the first Tuesday of each month.

It doesn't have to have a card. The world's second-largest oil company **Exxon Corporation**

We must keep in mind that a card program, no matter what industry you are in, will not be compensation for bad service or dirty floors or dirty hotel rooms, bad pricing and so on. *It's a reinforcement of the business basics. It's not a* replacement *for the business basics.*

—BRIAN WOOLF, PRESIDENT OF RETAIL STRATEGY CENTER, IN COLLOQUY

Forget about the sales you hope to make and concentrate on the service you want to render.

—HARRY BULLIS,
FORMER CEO OF
GENERAL MILLS

recently sent newspaper subscribers a free key chain adorned with their trademarked tiger. As part of the company's "This Month's Treat" program, the key chain entitled customers to a new deal each month at Exxon gas stations. For example, in August 1998, the key chain and a quarter bought a choice of a cup of coffee, a fountain drink, or a can of soda.

———— ● ————

Baby Boomers may remember the gas station promotions of the 1960s. Free and discounted sets of steak knives, glasses, and dinnerware, completed a piece per visit, drove repeat business. The idea is still thriving at **Farm Fresh** supermarkets where shoppers can accumulate a discounted set of Oneida's Immaculate cookware one piece per week. Each weekly Farm Fresh ad flier features a coupon for a new pot or pan.

———— ● ————

What about trading stamps? Recently, **Ukrop's** was giving away trading stamps redeemable for Roma Gourmet Cookware to build repeat sales. Customers receive one stamp for every $5 spent on groceries and each 20-stamp card earns another discounted piece in the set.

———— ● ————

Ukrop's also uses its Value Customer card (UVC) to manage its repeat programs. This one was created in conjunction with General Mills: Buy 12 boxes of any General Mills cereal and get a $5 Ukrop's gift certificate. Sound like a lot of cereal? Customers get a full year to accumulate the total, and as always, Ukrop's keeps track of purchases and mails the gift certificate automatically.

And this, too: The grocer's "Cookie Dough" program. For every three packages of Nabisco cookies, Sweet Crispers, or Honeymaid graham crackers purchased between April 1 and December 31, 1999, with a UVC card, customers get $1 in "Cookie Dough," good on any purchase at the store. All automatic.

———— • ————

Let's talk turkey. Many grocers use some variation of this one: Customers who spent at least $500 in a set period prior to Thanksgiving '98 at **Ukrop's** received a gift certificate good for a free 12- to 14-pound turkey. And there's a good twist for folks who just don't eat that much. Seniors and singles who signed up for the offer and spent $250 got a certificate good for $5 off on a frozen or prepared turkey. And, since the program was tracked using the company's frequent buyer card, it was automatic—no saving receipts, etc.

———— • ————

Lompoc, California–based **Mi Amore Pizza & Pasta** offers a club card of its own to customers. Purchase the $2 card and earn points each time you dine at the Italian restaurant. The points can be redeemed for menu items, specialty prizes, and even discounts at other area merchants.

———— • ————

Classy **Kravet,** a purveyor of decorative fabrics and furniture to the interior design trade, named its frequent buyer program "Rewards of Style." Interior designers and architects earn points for purchasing the company's products for use in their client's homes and offices. The points can be redeemed for a bevy of rewards, including a trip to a well-known spa, tickets to the World Series, and of course, designer furniture.

*Do you know what it costs when your company loses a customer? The lifetime value of a loyal **Cadillac** customer is $332,000. At **Pizza Hut,** a lifetime customer is worth up to $8,000.*

———— ● ————

3M Pharmaceuticals created 3M Plus Rewards for its druggist customers in New Zealand, where the choice of drug brand is made by pharmacists, not doctors. The program gives members additional product discounts and also awards points redeemable for a wide variety of goods and money-saving coupons at area retailers.

———— ● ————

Some products, such as earthmoving machinery, just don't lend themselves to frequent buyer cards. So, when Tokyo, Japan–based **Komatsu Ltd.** wants to encourage its customers to upgrade from iron (heavy equipment) to big iron (even heavier equipment), it puts them in the operator's seat. For example, Komatsu recently invited customers to its Chattanooga, Tennessee, testing ground. In addition to providing plenty of hands-on use, the world's second-largest construction equipment maker picked up the transportation, lodging, and meals for its customers during their stay.

———— ● ————

Heavy equipment dealer **Equipco** and manufacturer **Hitachi** teamed up to show off their wares. They wined and dined repeat customers on a two-day junket to the Hard Rock Café in Las Vegas. However, the highlight of trip, according to one customer, was the opportunity to run big iron in the desert just outside a U.S. Air Force base, where jets and helicopters provided an unintended air show.

BUY IT BACK

Do you really want customers to keep coming back? Then, buy back what they purchased in the first place. Sound crazy? Isn't that how auto leasing works? A car buyer purchases a car for a fixed time period, and then returns it. The car company "buys" it back by discounting the payments to reflect the car's value when it is returned. Oh yeah, and see you in 36 months for a new one!

————————— ● —————————

North Sioux City, South Dakota–based **Gateway, Inc.,** the world's second-largest direct marketer of personal computers, will buy your outdated Gateway if you'll buy a new one from them. Gateway's Obsolescence Protection plan is available under their Your:)Ware program and allows buyers to trade in today's model toward a new one in two or four years. The company uses the current Orion Blue Book to determine your current computer's value and the trade-in amount can only be used toward another Gateway system. That's locking in repeat business.

————————— ● —————————

Every community seems to have at least one used paperback store. In our town, that store is the **Book Exchange of Williamsburg** and, like similar stores, its entire business is built around a variation on frequent-buyer programs. The Book Exchange uses a barter system to keep customers coming back to the store. Customers trade in their used paperbacks and in return, get store credits equaling one-quarter of the books' cover price. The credits can be applied to the store's stock, which is resold at half the cover price. The result: a profitable business built on the repurchase of "consumed" products and repeat customers.

————————— ● —————————

St. Louis-based **Chapter One Books** sells new and used books, specializing in romance novels, westerns, and mysteries. It keeps customers com-

> You want your customers for life. Companies must treat their customers with that in mind.
>
> —ALLAN KARL,
> VICE PRESIDENT OF
> PRISCOMM

ing back with a buy-back program with a twist: Once customers have read the books they purchase in the store, Chapter One will buy them back for cash or store credits. An inexpensive paperback, for example, might bring 5¢ cash or a 50¢ store credit. Not a lot, but enough of a rebate to keep customers recycling their books.

SPECIAL CUSTOMERS— SPECIAL REWARDS

In the last chapter, we suggested you reward every customer, that you treat all of them as if they were your best customers. Now, we'll add an amendment to that rule: Figure out who your best customers are and treat them even better.

For many companies, customers' purchasing habits will follow the Pareto Principle: Roughly 80% of the revenue in any given business is generated by the top 20% of its customers. That top 20%, which represents the company's most active customers, should be rewarded for their exceptional loyalty.

Plenty of companies agree and they recognize and reward their best customers in a wide range of ways. Many say thanks with outright gifts and celebrations. Others make sure that their reward programs are geared toward higher levels of spending, and still others create special programs for the most elite of their customers.

Here are lots of good ideas to build even better relationships with the people who are instrumental in your business success.

GIVE THEM A PRESENT

How about sending gifts on your birthday? To celebrate its tenth anniversary, Montana-based pager and radio equipment company **Cosner Comtech, Inc.** sent its top customers a thank-you note with their choice of four free accessories worth up to $40.

What do you do with the samples your vendors send you? At **The Business Reader,** we run a quarterly listing of customers by sales volume and pass on the advance and review copies of the latest business books the nation's publishers send us, along with a thank-you note for their patronage. It is a low-cost way to reward great customers where everyone wins: our customers get free books, publishers get advance copies of their new books to readers, and we get happy customers . . . and, when a book captures interest, additional orders!

Bloomingdale's by Mail woos its regular customers with a surprise thank you now and then. One mailing started with "A Gift for You with our thanks." It went on to explain that "you're one of our favorite customers." The payoff: a free one-year gift subscription to *Food & Wine* magazine.

Microsoft Corporation recently introduced the bimonthly *Insider* newsletter, a free publication that it sends to the "extremely valued Microsoft customer who has registered numerous products with us." Much more than a merchandising ploy, the newsletter thanked customers for continually choosing Microsoft and featured useful articles describing how to get the most from the company's software.

Retailers are beginning to understand that certain customers, those who are very loyal, are worth a great deal more than just the casual customer.

—ROBIN LANIER,
INTERNATIONAL
MASS RETAIL ASSOCIATION

—— ● ——

Inc. magazine reported how **Leegin Creative Leather Products** rewarded representatives of its top retail accounts with a business trip to the Far East. But, it was the pictures that this leather accessory maker snapped of their unsuspecting guests that made the return home so memorable. The company turned the pictures into postcards and mailed them to their guests' top 2,500 customers, generating new orders and requests for special displays and seminars.

—— ● ——

Recognition makes a fine gift. Carlstadt, New Jersey–based gas station and convenience store equipment distributor **Ten Hoeve Bros., Inc.** throws an annual holiday dinner for its customers. The biggest customers are presented with plaques of appreciation. Ten Hoeve makes two of each—one for the customer and one to display in their own offices.

—— ● ——

New Jersey–based water and soil testing service **Aqua-Protech Labs** celebrates the holidays and its best customers at the same time at its annual party. In 1998, customers and staff dined at the elegant Pegasus Restaurant high atop the well-known Meadowlands Racetrack. The year's biggest client was called to center stage to receive a case of fine wine as his company name went up in lights on the racetrack's big screens. Then he was summoned to the track to crown the winning horse in the next race.

—— ● ——

The sixth largest U.S. airline, **U.S. Airways Group,** often goes the extra mile for members of its frequent flyer programs. In addition to deeply discounting seating upgrades at the gate, the airline is known for the free upgrades it

> **Men who drive sharp bargains with their customers, acting as if they never expected to see them again, will not be mistaken. They never will see them again as customers.**
>
> **—P. T. Barnum**

often offers. Coach passengers who ask at the gate can find themselves in first-class, compliments of the carrier.

———— ● ————

The **Crowne Plaza** hotel chain offers its frequent guests a perk that is well suited to the flight schedules of business travelers. All 60 of the hotels participate in the "Your Room Is Ready" program, which allows check-ins as early as 7:00 A.M. and checkouts up to 3:00 P.M.

REWARD HIGH FREQUENCY

Frequency marketing programs can also be set to single out your best customers. Supermarket chain **Winn-Dixie** reached out to its best customers recently with a five-week program. Customers who spent at least $50 per week for a total of $250 in a five-week period were rewarded with a $50 gift certificate.

———— ● ————

While many credit cards rebate a fixed amount of every purchase regardless of frequency, **The Chase Manhattan Corporation's** Cashbuilder Gold Visa card purposely appeals to the high-volume user. If you charge at least $200 per month, the Cashbuilder Reward Plan automatically refunds 1% of purchases and cash advances and 10% of interest payments. The company generates a check only when the rebate amount reaches $500 or after three years, whichever comes first.

———— ● ————

The **Jones New York** factory store chain invites customers to join the CAP (Customer Appreciation Program) by simply signing up on a mailing list. CAP participants receive regular mailings from Jones New York that include

Not all customers are created equal.

—Dale Renner,
Andersen Consulting

coupons and advise them of upcoming sales events. But, it takes $750 in purchases to trigger rewards. Once the floor is reached, customers receive gift certificates for clothing in any of the chain's specialty stores including Career, Sports, and Executive.

—————— • ——————

What do frozen cakes and plumbing supplies have in common? Vacations. If you are a sales rep at a distributor of the gourmet cakes made by the **Bubbles Baking Company,** you could be flying free. Bubbles uses American Airlines Something Special Flight and Gift Certificates to reward the reps who sell the most cakes. Distributors' salespeople get points, tracked monthly, for each product sold. At year-end, those who accumulate between 25,000 and 45,000 points get to redeem them for roundtrip airline tickets.

—————— • ——————

New Jersey's **Palermo Plumbing** also gives away vacations to its biggest customers. Rather than just offer one trip to one winner, Palermo offers several tiers of trips based on buying levels. What most of them have in common, though, is that they go to warm places during New Jersey's cold winter. Says one loyal customer, "Why should I use two plumbing suppliers when my business could add up to a free trip at Palermo?"

—————— • ——————

New York City–based **Bliss** has created two automatic frequency programs—one for the customers of its spa and the other for the buyers of its Bliss Out spa products division. It's a small business, so Bliss keeps it simple. They keep track of the "BlissMiles," but send no statements, etc., to the customers. Each dollar spent at the company converts to a mile, and

What's Loyalty Worth?

- In insurance, adding just 5% in retention results in a 60% profit jump.
- In employer services, adding just 4% in retention results in a 21% profit jump.
- In banking, adding just 5% in retention results in a 40% profit jump.

—BAIN & COMPANY STUDY

The only profit center is the customer.

—PETER DRUCKER

starting at 1,500 miles, they can be redeemed for free and discounted products or services.

———————•———————

Given the wide availability of greeting cards in other outlets, customers who make special stops at card stores need encouragement. **Hallmark** recognized this and created the Hallmark Gold Crown Card. To sign up, customers are asked to fill out a short form of standard information during checkout. Subsequent purchases at the Gold Crown chain earn 10 points for every dollar spent, plus an additional 25 points for each greeting card purchased. Earn between 200 and 4,200 per quarter, and the company sends a gift certificate worth up to $20 off future purchases.

———————•———————

For those of us who just can't resist office supply stores, superstore chain **Staples, Inc.** has created the Dividends reward program. Dividends rewards customers based on the volume of their spending. It takes a minimum of $50 in purchases to activate the card, and after that each purchase is tracked. Spend between $250 and $600 per quarter and earn between 1 and 2½% on future purchases. By the way, Staples excludes big-ticket items (such as computers, printers, copiers, and fax machines) from the program.

———————•———————

Fly out of the **Newport News/Williamsburg International Airport** (NNWI) at least six times per year, and you're qualified for membership in the Business Aviator Club. Members earn a flight credit for each time they fly out of the airport. Points are redeemable for free parking days, coffee, newspapers, invitations to quarterly luncheons, and free business services on departure day including faxes, copies, and meeting room usage.

———————•———————

The Hertz Corporation, world leader in the rental car industry, charges $50 for membership in its #1 Club Gold program, which takes members directly to their ready-and-running cars—no check-in, no fuss. In 1999, however, instead of a bill for the membership, select repeat customers were pleasantly surprised to get a personalized letter informing them that their membership was automatically extended for another year at no cost.

CREATE ELITE PROGRAMS

Another way to make special customers feel special is to give them their own reward programs. **NationsBank,** recently merged with Bank of America, created the Advantage program for clients whose combined business with the bank adds up to a total that is substantially above average. Advantage customers receive free checks, a free safe-deposit box, free access to online PC banking, and preferred loan rates. In addition, normal fees for services such as stop payments, money orders, and incoming wire transfers are waived.

———————•———————

Most customers join **Quality Paperback Book Club** (QPB) for its generous signing bonus that does not require future purchases. So why buy more? One reason is the club's "QPB Preferred Member" program, which automatically kicks in after you have purchased six books. Preferred members get double the bonus points for their purchases, an additional free book, exclusive discounts, a dedicated

If you don't work these programs, or you ignore them, you're dead.

—JIM LAIDERMAN, EQUIFAX NATIONAL DECISION SYSTEMS

Here's one from the go-figure department: A survey of 11 banks in the U.K. conducted by the London publication Cus-tomer Loyalty Today found that a 5% increase in customer retention paid off with an 85% gain in bank deposit profits and a 75% rise in credit card profits. The same study found that only 44% of those surveyed thought that retaining customers was critical to their companies.

toll-free hotline, discounted rush delivery, and free gift wrap on larger orders.

———— • ————

Swissotel Management Ltd. created Club Swiss Gold for the top 20% of its guests—ranked by revenues. Members receive upgrades whenever available, free breakfast, and complimentary room guarantees. They are also asked to complete a form specifying any and all of their preferences, so they will be consistently well treated at all of the chain's 21 properties.

———— • ————

High rollers at **Harrah's Entertainment, Inc.'s** Tunica, Mississippi, casino are offered membership in an elite group simply known as "Premier." Members receive all the benefits of Harrah's Total Gold Program in addition to those little extras, like a massage chair with a secure storage area for personal belongings when playing the slots in their own exclusive area. And, telephones—with speed dialing for refreshments—should they need to reach out and touch someone.

———— • ————

American Airlines added levels to its AAd-vantage frequent flyer program with the Executive Platinum card for customers who log over 100,000 miles each year on the company's flights. These loyal customers receive special services including a dedicated customer service desk, deferred mileage expiration, fewer black-out dates, early upgrade confirmation, and several other perks.

———— • ————

Delta Air Lines, Inc. created the SkyPrivi-leges Plus program for businesses spending be-tween $40,000 and $250,000 per year on air travel. Meet certain spending thresholds each quarter and there is a barrel-full of benefits that include service discounts, access to SkyPrivileges Corporate Booking (an automated self-booking service), free domestic flight upgrades and tickets, and Silver or Gold Medallion frequent flyer status for all the company's travelers.

———— ● ————

Regular customers of **Federated Department Stores, Inc.'s** Bloomingdale's chain who reach a certain spending level are invited to join that company's preferred customer program. The program revolves around a Bloomingdale's Premier Visa credit card that is free of charge and offers the following benefits:

- Gift certificates are earned at the rate of 6% of all Bloomingdale's purchases and 3% of all Premier Visa purchases everywhere else
- Unlimited complimentary gift wrap
- Exclusive quarterly discount days offering additional discounts of 10 to 15%
- Free shipping and handling on all *Bloomingdale's by Mail, Ltd.* catalog purchases
- Free UPS pickup on returns—no questions asked
- Seasonal private sales and bonus certificates to add to the savings

———— ● ————

Federated also owns the Macy's chain, which created Club Macy's for its frequent buyers. All Macy's credit card holders are automatically enrolled at the Preferred Level of membership, but those who charge between $500 and $2,500 annually are Premier members, and those who charge over $2,500 belong to the President's Club.

All levels enjoy special shopping days, early notice of sale days and a 10% discount on their

> Be it furniture, clothes, or healthcare, many industries today are marketing nothing more than commodities—no more, no less. What will make the difference in the long run is the care and feeding of customers.
>
> —DANIEL SCROGGIN

The best place to learn about frequency marketing is your desk. **Frequency Marketing, Inc.'s** Colloquy Web site (www.colloquy.com) features hundreds of case studies, interviews with experts, book reviews, message boards and live discussion areas, article reprints . . . you name it. The free registration yields full access.

first shopping day with their new card. The Premier Level receives the additional benefits of a quarterly newsletter, three annual Premier Days with discounts of up to 15%, and a Visa card that earns gift certificates and free gift wrapping. Finally, the President's Club earns all that and more with free alterations, free local delivery, and its own toll-free customer service number.

————— ● —————

Buy regularly from **Spiegel, Inc.** catalogs and the $3-billion mail-order giant automatically enrolls you in its Elite program. Elite members are welcomed with a $10 gift certificate good on their next $50 purchase and a supply of "priority" stickers, so Spiegel employees easily recognize their orders. Members receive free gift wrapping, exclusive sales, one-time deals including free shipping on Christmas returns, and expedited mail- and phone-order processing.

————— ● —————

Book your second cruise on the **Holland America Line** and when you arrive in your room, you will find a gift and a welcome letter announcing that you are a freshly minted member of the line's Society of Honorary Mariners. In addition, if finer accommodations are still available at cruise time, Society members are offered complimentary upgrades. The policy thrilled friends of ours, who returned from an Alaska Inside Passage Cruise reporting a wholly unexpected upgrade to one of the ship's largest staterooms complete with a private balcony, a $2,000 value.

————— ● —————

San Francisco–based discount broker **The Charles Schwab Corporation** grew to over $2 billion in annual sales by offering no-frills investment transactions, but that doesn't mean they don't recognize their best customers. Customers who make over 48 trades a year are enrolled in the "Schwab 500." Henceforth, they get treated to some of the services of full-priced, full service brokerages, such as a dedicated group of employees to handle their accounts and research services.

———— • ————

Buy 5,000 gallons of gas a year from **Oura Oil,** and you are service station royalty. These most respected members of the Japanese company's Five-Up Club get a special club card that alerts attendants to the customer's higher status. They respond with extra services, such as vacuuming the car or replacing the windshield wiper fluid, free of charge.

———— • ————

Pier 1 Imports maintains a three-tiered, credit card–based frequent buyer program. Any customer can sign up for the card. Spend $500 during at least two shopping trips per year and get upgraded to Gold status with a 20% off coupon. Spend $1,000 on three or more store visits per year and get upgraded to Platinum. Platinum members get discounted shopping days each month and gift certificates for 10% of their purchases beginning at $1,000.

———— • ————

New Jersey–based insurer **The Chubb Corporation** is one of only a handful of insurers in America that is pursuing the property insurance business of the roughly 6% of Americans who own assets worth $1 million or more, over and above their homes. The company has designed high-end policies that minimize paperwork, while extending limits on expenses for temporary living quarters and expanded replacement coverage for goods that standard policies limit,

> Guess what? Loyal customers like dealing with the same people.
>
> —BARRY GIBBONS, IN *IF YOU WANT TO MAKE GOD REALLY LAUGH, SHOW HIM YOUR BUSINESS PLAN*

What determines how much a long-term customer is potentially worth is whether you have earned his loyalty. This loyalty is so important that it should be factored in when evaluating the true net worth of a company.

—C. BRITT BEEMER IN
PREDATORY MARKETING

such as wine, jewelry, and collectible cars. Chubb's Masterpiece policy also offers discounts for second homes.

————— ◉ —————

Professional photographers spend between $150,000 and $500,000 per year on photo finishing and Iowa-based **McKenna Professional Imaging** has created a series of programs designed to capture larger shares of their business. The company offers a free business education in its Management and Accounting for Portrait Studios program, teaches marketing in its Portrait Value Plan, and will even make prospecting calls on behalf of their photographer clients. All free, to customers who agree to give McKenna 80% of their processing business.

————— ◉ —————

The Colonial Williamsburg Foundation divides its donors into levels of giving, offering progressively higher thanks at each increased level. In the upper range, The Raleigh Tavern Society is itself organized into three levels: the entry is at the $5,000 mark; next is the Apollo Room Circle at $7,500; and, finally, Keeper of the Key at $10,000. All donors, from $35 in annual giving on up, receive thank-yous, such as in the nonprofit's monthly magazine.

————— ◉ —————

Membership has its privileges . . . and highest membership receives the highest privileges. **American Express Company's** Platinum Card is the créme de la créme of its offerings and comes with a hefty annual fee of $300. But, explained Amex spokeswoman Judy Tenzer to *Worth* magazine, "If a member uses each perk once a year, they essentially save more than $7,000." They include:

- a free companion ticket worth up to $3,000 to purchasers of a full-fare international ticket in first or business class
- free access to the airport VIP lounges of two major airlines
- reservations at over 200 restaurants that are notoriously difficult to get into
- free subscription to glossy magazine *Departures,* exclusively written for Platinum cardholders

Recently, the American Express Fine Hotels & Resorts Program offered Platinum cardholder programs for members at such luxurious inns as Baden Baden in Germany and the Meadowood in Napa Valley, among others. Cardholders were treated to a complimentary room upgrade if available on check-in, breakfast for two each day, and a guaranteed late checkout of 4:00 P.M., plus an extra program amenity according to location.

They also enjoy access to the exclusive *Platinum Destinations* program offering exotic travel experiences and earning double *Membership Rewards* program points. Recently, skiing in the Canadian Rockies was offered with accommodations at the Banff Springs Hotel or Chateau Lake Louise. Goodies on the six-night trip included a $75 resort credit, five lift passes for unlimited skiing at the three area ski resorts, and free transfers.

Special events are covered in the *By Invitation Only* program, which gives cardholders access to events such as Miami's Orange Bowl, along with club suite tickets and a tailgate party. There are also merchandise specials: Recently, those customers who used their Platinum cards to buy a suit at Brooks Brothers received a free made-to-measure shirt.

Treat the customer as an appreciating asset.

—TOM PETERS IN
THRIVING ON CHAOS

8

MAKE IT EASY

Here is a common-sense maxim that all vendors should adopt: Make it easy for your customers to do business with you. It sounds fundamental. It *is* fundamental. But, just because it is fundamental does not mean that everyone gets it. Think about it for a minute, and you can probably come up with a half-dozen examples of companies that are tough to work with. We certainly can.

"Making it is easy" is a wonderful differentiating factor for your business. And, you might be surprised at how high it ranks among your customers' priorities.

There are two basic principles for making it easy:

1. Simplify every customer interface.
2. Make it convenient to do business with you.

"Keep it simple" is an especially good mantra for today's high-speed world. Customers appreciate simplicity. It is more efficient, more effective, and there is an elegance to simplicity to which people unfailingly respond. Even if you make products that require an advanced technical education to use, anyone should be able to figure out how to order them.

Convenience counts just as much. A business that takes into account its customers' convenience keeps them coming back by giving them back more of their most valuable possession: Time. Offer your customers all the options, services, and purchasing hours you can. Give them the ability to do business where and when they want.

KEEP IT SO SIMPLE

Think KISS. Polite translation: Keep it so simple. Shipping giant **United Parcel Service** did just that when it created the reusable overnight delivery envelope. It is an idea that businesses sending documents requiring signatures—such as banks, brokerage firms, or attorneys—have to love. With the new package, their clients simply sign the paperwork, put it back in the same envelope, reseal the special flap with a second strip of adhesive, and return it. As simple as can be, *and* UPS captures the return business.

UPS also offers its customers free UPS OnLine Office software. The software stores addresses, prints labels, automatically computes shipping charges, and tracks packages. Further, it will e-mail your customers with their package information, such as delivery date, tracking numbers, contents, weight, and other details.

And for the triple play, there's the UPS Document Exchange program. It will send any digital document over the Internet in a universally readable file, at the level of security chosen by the customer. And, as with anything sent by the small package specialist, tracking and delivery confirmation is available.

Two words: Negative Response. All the mail-order clubs use it because it is simple and smart. We'll use Camp Hill, Pennsylvania-based **Quality Paperback Book Club** (QPB) as an example: About once a month, QBC sends out a thick envelope packed with information on new paperbacks and a recommendation for one book that they think is an especially worthy read. If you want the book, *do nothing* and soon it arrives at your door. In other words, the sales agreement is implied in the lack of action. That's negative response.

Of course, the problem for customers with negative response is that if they do *not* want the product, it requires an action to stop the automatic shipment. (It's inconvenient in a world where convenience counts.) No one has completely solved that problem, but the system used by **Columbia House's Classical Club** comes close. If you want their Selection of the Month, do nothing. But if you don't, forget about the time and cost of mailing a response. Members may decline selections via the Web or by calling on a touch-tone phone.

Here's a twist on negative response: Recently, *Allure* magazine was one of 300 publications offered to American Express customers. The first year was free, but after that, the renewal price of $12 is automatically charged to the customer's American Express account. Will subscribers find paying easier than canceling?

The **Richmond Times-Dispatch** offers subscribers a Vacation Pak. Let the newspaper know when you are going on vacation and it will automatically hold the papers until you

> I am the world's worst salesman; therefore, I must make it easy for people to buy.
>
> —F. W. WOOLWORTH

> **Be everywhere, do everything, and never fail to astonish the customer.**
>
> —R. H. MACY'S MOTTO

get back and then resume service and deliver the issues in a "nice neat Vacation Pak" upon your return.

———— ● ————

You can blame Seattle-based **Starbucks Corporation** for the coffee bar craze, but the $1 billion company has made keeping fresh coffee much easier with its Encore delivery service. Sign up for the program and every five weeks fresh coffee automatically arrives at your door. Freshness is guaranteed with a replacement or refund promise, and Starbucks also offers a free 10-cup coffeemaker as a signing bonus.

———— ● ————

Des Moines, Iowa–based **Gevalia Kaffe** offers a similar program with limited edition coffees that are only available once a year. Gevalia sells coffees directly to their customers by subscription. The initial offer is quite tempting: Two half-pound packages of exotic coffee, free mugs, an insulated carafe in a choice of colors, and a newsletter all for only $5. After that, every three months, subscribers will automatically receive four half-pound packages of another rare coffee along with a bill for $6.25 to $6.95 per half-pound.

———— ● ————

Salad in a bag is the best thing since sliced bread. Salinas, California's **Farm Fresh Express** revolutionized the lettuce business by cleaning, shredding, and bagging greens for customers. Do people appreciate it? Just take a look at how much space is now devoted to these products in your local supermarket.

———— ● ————

American Airlines has made it easier than ever for its frequent flyers traveling on e-tickets to board their flights. Rather than waiting on lines at the ticket counters or gates for clearance, Platinum and Gold AAdvantage members swipe their frequent-flyer card or the credit card used to buy the ticket into the new AAccess Boarding Unit. Security clearance is processed, a "boarding entitlement" printed, and the passenger enplanes.

———————●———————

Capital One's Platinum Miles*One* VISA card makes it easier to earn free tickets in the first place. It rewards customers with generic air miles that may be used on any U.S.-based airline at any time for any seat. No confining lists of partners, no blackout dates, no restrictions.

———————●———————

The world's leading issuer of credit cards, **Citicorp** gave the same idea a new curve with its Driver's Edge VISAs and MasterCards. The cards' 2% rebates on purchases can be used toward any make or model car in America. By the way, the rebate is capped at $500 per year and $1,500 on each purchase or lease.

———————●———————

Sometimes customers, and companies, get tangled up in too many programs. **Marriott International, Inc.** combined three incentive programs into one and simplified everyone's lives. The revamped Rewards program tracks room nights, vacations, etc., automatically and can be used at the 1,300 participating hotels in the Marriott family. It earns 10 points for every dollar spent, and pays out with a free room night after approximately 15 nights.

———————●———————

The **Colonial Williamsburg Foundation** (CW) makes it easy for its supporters to give with its own Platinum Visa Card issued by First USA. When CW patrons use the card, a percentage of

Make everything as simple as possible, but not simpler.

—ALBERT EINSTEIN

the charges go directly to Colonial Williamsburg at no additional cost to customers.

———— ⚫ ————

The Smithsonian Institution knows a good idea when it sees one, and signed up for its own Novus card. For the civic-minded, each use of the card pays cash back to the Smithsonian. And, cardholders win, too. Every $100 in purchases earns one point towards savings bonds. Customers automatically receive a $50 U.S. Savings Bond each time they accrue 50 points.

———— ⚫ ————

How about automatic deductions for religious donations? **The Lutheran Brotherhood** has created the Simply Giving program that automatically debits your bank account for whatever amount you choose to regularly give. Feel strange not pitching in during church? The program offers I-gave-electronically stickers so you don't look less-than-generous on your day of worship.

———— ⚫ ————

First Union National Bank is keeping customers coming back—even when they move away. Instead of requiring customers to close their bank account and reopen them—perhaps, with a competitor—in a new city, First Union does the work itself, simply transferring the existing accounts or setting up new ones when necessary. It does the same for loans, credit card accounts, and even investments.

———— ⚫ ————

The **American Automobile Association** came up with this fine example of simplicity. Get your cell phone service from the organization and it comes with a special "AAA Button." Forget about looking up the number if your car breaks down; just push the button and you're connected.

It pays to call Ohio-based auto insurer **The Progressive Corporation** the moment you have a fender-bender. The company may well immediately dispatch an SUV equipped with a portable accident processing system. Once it arrives on the scene, a claims agent estimates the damage, arranges for your transportation, and cuts you a check—on the spot.

Smart cards are coming of age. **American Express, Continental Airlines,** and **Hilton Hotels** (there's a strong partnership bundle) are testing a frequent traveler card that holds personalized information in an embedded computer chip. In addition to being a credit card, the card "knows" and conveys such details as frequent flyer numbers, hotel room requirements, and preferred airplane seating. It can also be used in designated terminals at airports and hotels to allow the traveler to avoid ticket counters and front desks.

The traditional gift certificate has always been an inconvenience. Customers must either figure out what they can buy for exactly $50 or $100 or deal with the often-interminable bookkeeping. Enter the electronic gift card. Tony retailer **The Neiman Marcus Group, Inc.** solved that problem with smart gift cards that work like credit cards. Pay for your purchases until the credit amount is simply used up. Neiman's even offers cards specifically designed for special occasions and as corporate gifts complete with the purchaser's logo or message.

Sears, Roebuck & Co. gave the idea a creative twist when it introduced an electronic gift card for back-to-school spending. Parents purchase the electronic cards for the specific amount they want to spend and then give the card to their kids to make their own back-to-school purchases. The children don't have to carry cash or their parents' credit cards, but can still shop on their own.

———— ⬤ ————

Bloomingdale's picked up on the electronic gift cards and offers them in amounts from $10 to $500. Even better, customers don't have to go to the store to get them. The cards can be purchased over the phone and online.

———— ⬤ ————

American Express Gift Cheques aren't quite as high-tech, but the folks you give them to can use them in a lot more places. Available in $25, $50, and $100 denominations, Gift Cheques are sold at American Express Travel Service Offices, AAA, banks, and credit unions. And, like the company's Travelers Checks, Gift Cheques are refundable if lost or stolen.

———— ⬤ ————

No matter what kind of gift certificate you create, if your customers don't know it is available, you won't sell them. You can't miss 'em at Bisbee, Arizona's **Main Street Antiques.** A sample of the store's gift certificates is prominently displayed over the owner's desk in full view of the customers. It's an attention-grabber and conversation-starter because it is made out in the name of the ghost that supposedly haunts the store in the historic mining town.

———— ⬤ ————

Customers have come to expect automated phone systems at companies that get heavy phone traffic, such as banks and software makers. Now, they're popping up in some unexpected places: Dayton, Ohio's **Miami Valley Hospital** (MVH) improved its response to pa-

---

What Is a Customer?

A Customer is the most important person ever in this office . . . in person or by mail.

A Customer is not dependent on us . . . we are dependent on him.

A Customer is not an interruption of our work . . . he is the purpose of it. We are not doing a favor by serving him . . . he is doing us a favor by giving us the opportunity to do so.

A Customer is not someone to argue or match wits with. Nobody ever won an argument with a Customer.

A Customer is a person who brings us his wants. It is our job to handle them profitably to him and ourselves.

—VINTAGE SIGN AT L. L. BEAN HEADQUARTERS

tients with billing questions with a voice response system. Clients call the system, enter their account numbers, and receive current balances and other account information automatically. Should they need to speak with a customer service representative, the system transfers the call along with the already-retrieved account information.

———•———

The world's largest pizza chain **Pizza Hut, Inc.** knows what its home-delivery customers want before they even order! The chain's more than 10,000 stores sport computer systems that recognize customers by their phone numbers, so order takers can casually ask, "Do you want the usual?" And, that's about all the information they need because your usual delivery address is also in the computer. It just doesn't get any easier.

Or does it? If you are surfing the Web in Topeka, Kansas, and feel like a pizza, you just got lucky. Pizza Hut is testing www.pizzahut.com in that area and now, with a click of the delivery button and a little info, a hot pie is on the way.

———•———

Drive-thru fast food hadn't been perfected until **Wendy's International** improved the ordering process with a video screen. Now, when you can't understand a word the order taker is saying, you can read it instead. The technology reduces errors and makes Wendy's just a little more appealing than the competition.

———•———

But for how long? **Burger King Corporation** is testing an array of improvements in a new restaurant located in Reno, Nevada. It features automatic doors for easy carry-out, transparent bags to help reduce order errors, computer-activated and controlled broilers that cook the

The annual American Customer Satisfaction Index, which measures how happy consumers are with the goods and services they purchase, has declined in each of the last three survey years. Buck the trend.

food when it is ordered (not before), and surprise—drive-thru video screens that show the items you've ordered.

————— • —————

Each holiday season, **Harry & David** sends out their specialty food and gift catalogs en masse— just like every other cataloger. Unlike the others, however, this company's includes an order form with a list of the orders you placed last year, complete with the names and addresses of recipients and the gifts you gave each of them. Simply make any changes necessary and your holiday shopping is done.

————— • —————

Surprisingly for a government agency, the **Bureau for the Public Debt's** Treasury Direct program is simple to use as anything offered in the private sector. Forget about banks and brokers: If you regularly buy U.S. Treasury Bonds, Bills, and Notes, open an account with the Bureau. Then, simply fill out a form choosing the government securities you want to purchase, and the Bureau provides them directly to you. Better yet, no money changes hands until the issue date of the security when payment is electronically collected from the customer's designated account.

————— • —————

The **U.S. Treasury's** EasySaver program for saving bonds works the same way. Customers can use direct transfers from their bank accounts to the Treasury to buy savings bonds on a regular basis. The individual investor decides how much to transfer and on which days and months deductions are to be made. The program covers Series EE savings bonds and the newer Series I inflation-indexed savings bonds at face values of $50 to $10,000.

————— • —————

Need a ride? Simply call **1-800-LIMO-CENTER** from anywhere in North America and select cities in Europe, and you got it. Use an American Express card to pay for the service and earn one ride credit for every $50 charged. Get a free limo ride after 20 credits.

———— ◉ ————

The **Hertz Corporation** knows how to keep it simple, too. Rent a car from Hertz at any one of 16 major U.S. airports (soon to be over 50) including Atlanta, Newark, Boston, Denver, and Baltimore, and inside it you will find the Enhanced Computerized Driving Directions system free of charge. Directions are available in English, French, German, Italian, Japanese, and Spanish and are door-to-door to any street address within the original rental city's area.

———— ◉ ————

Walgreen Company makes prescription refills a snap with three systems: The Touch Tone Prefills system is a 24-hour automated phone system allowing customers to order prescription refills and specify the pickup time up to six days in advance; On-Line Prefills allows re-ordering online; and Auto Prefills automatically refills prescriptions when they are due and then calls customers to let them know that their order is ready.

———— ◉ ————

As We Change, a cataloger selling customized vitamins and supplements for women, offers its customers the Expressly Yours program. It's an automatic re-delivery system that makes sure customers never run out of their vitamins. The pricing and shipping fees are guaranteed to stay the same, so there are no billing surprises, only convenience and automatic repeat business.

———— ◉ ————

Anybody can cut
prices, but it takes
brains to produce a
better article.

—P. D. Armour

Sephora, a 176-store chain selling high-end cosmetics and perfumes, is turning the traditional selling environment on its head. Its model is hands-on, so clients can sample as many products as they choose before making a purchase. It's also hands-off because sales staff is salaried, eliminating the hard sell. And, the stock is arranged by product type, not by manufacturer.

————— • —————

Dayton, Ohio–based **ChemStation** keeps its customers coming back to its industrial detergents by making sure they never have to place a refill order. The company monitors its clients' usage patterns, forecasts when deliveries are needed, reorders the materials, and automatically refills the containers. In addition, each customer's detergent is specifically formulated for his or her application.

————— • —————

Napierville, Illinois–based **Nalco Chemical Company** automated the same idea. The maker of water-treatment chemicals created the Chem-Call—a just-in-time delivery plan powered by sensors in storage containers that notify the company when it's time for a refill. All the customer does is sign the delivery receipt.

————— • —————

If you have a complex product or service that potential customers might find initially intimidating, simplify it. New York City's **Metropolitan Opera** (Met) stages over 200 performances each year, and it wants to sell all of its 4,000 seats for each show. But, opera is not the widespread attraction it was a century or so ago, and since many are not presented in English, they can be tough for the uni-lingual patron to follow. The Met recently jumped that language barrier with a great idea—a discreet

translation system that runs subtitles in English on the back of the seat in front of you.

———— • ————

Realizing that buying original art can be as intimidating to new customers as opera (and lots more expensive), Soho, New York–based art gallery owner **Leah Poller** created the "Frame It, It's Yours" program. Poller invites customers to choose a favorite piece from among those on display in the gallery, and for the price of the framing alone, they can take it home and live with it for a few months. If customers still love it, they can buy it for a 30% discount from retail. However, if they find they made a mistake, the art can simply be returned.

———— • ————

Unless you have a mainframe computer sitting around, you've probably never heard of Hopkinton, Massachusetts–based **EMC Corporation,** the #1 maker of computer disk memory hard- and software. EMC's products are critical and complicated, so it eased its customers' minds by becoming one of the first companies to provide built-in remote maintenance. If there is a problem, the equipment automatically contacts EMC's customer service center. And, often the problems are solved even before customers become aware of them. Now, that's what we'd like to see in the new version of MS Windows.

———— • ————

Freightliner Corporation's big rigs include onboard computers that know when the trucks require service. The truck tells the manufacturer and the manufacturer alerts the owner.

———— • ————

In the it's-easier-than-winning department, the **Virginia Lottery** offered its regular customers an alternative to standing in line for tickets with

When the product is right, you don't have to be a great marketer.

—Lee Iacocca

its "Lotto-by-Mail" program. By mailing in a check with the subscription form, players participate in 26 to 104 draws. At two drawings per week, that's up to one year of no lines. And, subscriptions may even be purchased as gifts, provided both parties are over 18 years of age.

Corporate mergers and acquisitions are a regular occurrence these days, and they can be confusing to customers, so simplify them, too. During the merger of **Bank of America** and **NationsBank,** each credit card holder received a personalized letter keeping them up to date on the process and advising when the change in names and cards would be made. And as a thank you for being a customer and an incentive to remain an active one, a packet of special discount offers was thrown in.

Visitors to **SuperMarkets Online's** ValuPage Web site enter their zip code, complete a short survey, and can print the specials for markets in their area from their home computer. Customers take the page to the supermarket, buy any of the products listed, and the cashier simply scans the barcode at the top of the page. The supermarket's register adds up the savings and prints out a corresponding amount of "Web Bucks," which can be used to lower customers' grocery bills on their next visit to the market.

San Diego's **Road Runner Sports** makes shopping on its Web site simple with its "Shoe Dog." Answer a short questionnaire and turn Shoe Dog loose. It returns with the running shoes that exactly meet your specifications. Add in the unconditional guarantee and free two-day shipping, and it's a great formula to keep customers coming back.

———— ● ————

Mobil Oil simplifies the gas station with Speedpass. Using the same technology currently used on toll roads, Speedpass allows customers to gas up by simply flashing a tag that is hand-held or mounted on their cars. No cash, no card, and authorization is automatic. Mobil calls it "the fastest way to get gas."

MAKE IT CONVENIENT

No one knows who first said, "Time is of the essence," but everyone knows that convenience is as important as simplicity in building repeat business. Supermarket chain **Hy-Vee, Inc.** is coming on strong in the Midwest with over 200 markets in operation. It keeps customers coming back with a timesaving one-stop-shopping system that combines a food store with general merchandise and freshly prepared meals. Hy-Vee set up restaurants in their stores, giving their customers the choices of buying the ingredients for a meal, eating a meal in the store, or ordering take-out. They even have drive-up windows for those who are in a hurry. The markets also include bank branches, floral and photo shops, video rentals, dry cleaners, and other options to help their customers save time while doing errands and arranging meals.

———— ● ————

Sam's Club is a great place to shop for savings, but their membership card is not transferable—even among immediate family members. That makes it impossible to shop there without dragging along the cardholder, unless you are willing pay an additional card fee. Recently, however, Sam's offered its members a free spouse or secondary membership card for up to one year. Convenient for customers and smart for Sam's. When the secondary card is up for paid renewal, will the member really want to give it up?

———— • ————

Lots of catalog retailers maintain a free returns policy, but women's clothing cataloger **Boston Proper** takes it a step further with their "New Effortless Free Exchange Program." When your order arrives, the package includes a prepaid postal label. Don't want the merchandise? Reseal the box, slap on the label, and give it to your mail carrier.

———— • ————

Thrifty Rent-A-Car System, Inc. offers all its patrons a membership in the Blue Chip Express Rental Program. Forget about the usual paperwork at the time of rental, Blue Chip members simply sign the agreement and go. The drop-off process after the rental is just as easy and the membership is free.

———— • ————

Bethesda, Maryland–based **Marriott International, Inc.** knows that check-in and checkout are two times when customers are often inconvenienced. So, in its Marriott hotels, it implemented the "First Ten Program" designed to make the first 10 minutes in the hotel a pleasurable experience for customers. Now, an employee greets the guest at the door with the appropriate room key and escorts him/her directly to the room—no lines, no waiting, no hand-offs from employee to employee. In addition, checking out has been simplified with in-room video checkout services.

Marriott also offers "The Room That Works" program, which is designed specifically for the convenience of business travelers. These rooms include large desks, movable writing surfaces, special lighting, ergonomic chairs, extra outlets, and eye-level data ports. Where available, these specialized rooms are free for the asking—there is no additional charge.

———— ◈ ————

What's your car doing while you are flying off on business trips? If you are traveling out of Logan Airport in Boston and the car is parked at **Air Travelers Service Corporation's** lot, it could be getting washed, waxed, a safety inspection, new tires, and other auto services.

———— ◈ ————

Even in the era of free rides and loaners, sooner or later, every car owner ends up hanging around the service department. Anyone who has seen GM carmaker **Saturn's** recent ad campaign knows that when you choose to wait for your car at Saturn dealerships, there are a few bonuses. The service departments feature free snacks and beverages, television, and even *recent* magazines to help you pass the time.

———— ◈ ————

Auto dealer **Jaguar Cleveland's** waiting room is quiet with plenty of overstuffed comfortable furniture and a private restroom. There's coffee, television, and a couple of telephones so no one's waiting to get in touch with his or her office. Service personnel regularly offer updates on the cars' progress, provide quotes, and advise when a car is ready.

———— ◈ ————

Amazon.com is the king of convenience in the book industry, and we particularly like their gift card program. Buy a book as a gift and Amazon.com not only ships it for you, it also e-mails a greeting card with your message and the title of the book(s) to the recipient. Even better, it eliminates errors in shipping, with an online acceptance feature that asks the gift-getter to verify the proper shipping address

Heads-up customer service experts pay attention to the wait. They make the waiting area pleasant . . . Really smart service folks make the wait a part of the experience.

—T. Scott Gross
In *Outrageous!*

information, and allows Amazon to introduce itself to yet another potential customer.

———— ● ————

Our local **Williamsburg Motors, Inc.** doesn't provide a free loaner when you bring your vehicle in for service; and given the expense of such programs, we can't really blame them. But, the Ford dealer does the next best thing: It provides a complimentary shuttle service to and from your home or office while your car is in the shop.

———— ● ————

Companies need to give their customers easy, up-to-the-minute info just to stay competitive. San Jose, California–based **Viking Freight Systems** has eliminated the usual "it's somewhere between here and there" by giving its drivers scanners to log pickups and deliveries. Every piece of freight is tracked in real time, and the information is posted online for customers.

———— ● ————

Auction fans usually have to buy catalogs or visit the auction houses themselves to learn what's going on the block. Except at **Phoebus Auction Gallery,** a small regional auctioneer that puts its catalogs online. Phoebus clients can sign up for e-mail notification of the latest auctions and simply click on the mail's hot link to go directly to the auction catalog at www.phoebusauction.com. The catalogs include lot descriptions and many photos. Sotheby's, are you listening?

———— ● ————

Biztravel.com specializes in online travel arrangements for the frequent traveler who likes to stay in control. Customers set up a free account, filling out a detailed profile of preferences, frequent flyer numbers, and incentive goals, such as attaining gold or platinum status or earning that free trip. Biztravel.com takes it from there, recommending the flights and hotels best suited to the customer for each specific trip, making the reservations, and delivering the tickets.

———————— • ————————

Now, how about house-hunting? New York City realty firm **Corcoran Group** uses the Web to post digital photos of its properties, along with floor plans, square footage, and other detailed information. Clients preview the properties on their own and elect to visit only those that work for them. The results are good for business: Corcoran has found that the average online shopper buys after physically visiting four properties; clients who respond to newspaper ads see approximately 14 properties before buying.

———————— • ————————

And, registering for classes. Students at the **University of Minnesota** (UMN) no longer need to spend hours standing on line to sign up for classes only to find them full when their turn comes up. UMN students now go online to sign up for classes from their homes or dorms. Online services also include admission applications, course catalogs, and billing info.

———————— • ————————

Postage meter giant **Pitney Bowes** is busy making a trip to the post office a thing of the past. With the company's Personal Post option, your postage meter will refill itself over the telephone. Dial in the proper number, indicate the amount of postage you want, and the meter is refilled in a minute or two.

———————— • ————————

When systems get buggy, shopping online can get inconvenient, too. No troubles at

1800USAHOTELS's Web site, however. Customers having difficulty making reservations on the site can simply click the call-back button. They enter their phone number and a message, and a customer service rep quickly calls them.

————— ● —————

Have you ever asked for that perfect garment in your size and color and gotten a shrug from the salesperson in return? (Yes, that's a rhetorical question.) Not customers in **Bloomingdale's** fur department. If Bloomingdale's does not have one of their coats in the correct size, they track it down without obligation and phone the customer when it comes in. One shopper told us that the staff even offered to gather furs from other stores in her size and give her a private showing.

————— ● —————

Speaking of furs, taking them in for summer storage is an annual inconvenience. Except with **Virgina's Silverman Furs.** The furrier keeps customers coming back by coming to the furs. Representatives of the store fill its cold storage vaults by setting up shop for a day or two in outlying towns, thus capturing business that would usually be sent by local dry cleaners or department stores to larger regional storage facilities.

————— ● —————

Wondering if it's worth the time to attend that author reading at Los Angeles' **Dutton's Brentwood** bookstore? Get a preview. Dutton's signed up with BookTalk, an audio newsletter customers can access via telephone, so customers can hear authors in 15 categories reading their work for up to five minutes each.

————— ● —————

Cell phone maker **Uniden** recently released two new cordless phone models that do more than just make connections. In the space of one second, these phones check every long-distance database available at that moment and automatically connect your call using the lowest priced carrier. Known as the Uniden Long Distance Manager, there are no additional fees or paperwork, and all calls are charged on one monthly bill.

————— ● —————

Kinko's Inc. knows all about customer convenience. The Ventura, California–based copy center chain keeps customers by staying open 24 hours a day, 7 days a week including holidays. It provides the standard office needs such as scissors, paste, tables, and even free local telephone calls to customers; and employees are on hand to help figure out tougher questions, such as proper resume layout or letterhead and envelope designs.

————— ● —————

West Palm Beach, Florida, title insurance agency **Flagler Title** cut costs and eased its customer's paper load by replacing tall stacks of insurance and legal documents with a single CD-ROM. By the way, *Inc.* magazine reports that the company also substantially cut the $500 cost it incurred preparing the paper package.

————— ● —————

Catalog shoppers have to receive their order to find out how that outfit is going to look on them . . . or do they? Dodgeville, Wisconsin-based **Land's End** now offers "Your Personal Model" to its female online shoppers at www.landsend.com. Enter personal details such as hair color, weight, and rough estimates of shoulder, hip, and waist widths, and behold

an image of a person similar in size, shape, and coloring to you pops up on your screen. Now, simply click to dress the image for an advance look at yourself.

———— ● ————

How long? Irving, Texas–based **Neiman Marcus Mail Order** sped up its orders during the holiday season by sending each one via FedEx two-day delivery service at no additional charge. Less chance for damage and loss, happy customers, and an extended holiday shopping window for the company.

———— ● ————

Chesterfield Towne Center, a Chesterfield, Virginia, shopping mall, keeps parents coming back by keeping kids on call. A free beeper service is provided by the mall management in cooperation with ZAP, Inc., a communications retailer located on the premises. When parents and children are ready to split up, they go to the information desk in the food court where the kids are so equipped. When it's time to hit the road, parents simply stop by the information desk and beep 'em.

———— ● ————

The **IKEA** furniture and housewares chain made it convenient for parents to shop their stores over the 1998 holiday season with its "Story Time Saturday" program. Children ages three to eight were invited to attend any of several free storytelling sessions held from 10 A.M. to 3 P.M. Refreshments were served and participants received a complimentary audiocassette of stories of children's author Astrid Lindgren. Meanwhile, their parents got to do some uninterrupted shopping.

———— ● ————

Portland-based **Kindercare Learning Centers, Inc.** solves some common problems of working parents with extended hours. There is the Klubmates program, which caters to school-aged children before and after regular school hours and during holidays. The centers are staying open late on a regular schedule to allow parents the time to run errands, and even feature a late Friday night so parents can get some R&R.

———————●———————

Here's a convenience for us aging Baby Boomers. **Chase Manhattan** customers can sign up for the LensCard, a Visa or MasterCard with a built-in magnifying glass. Hold the corner of the credit card over the numbers on restaurant bills and voilà, they become legible even to those who misplaced their reading glasses. And, as long as the card is already out, why not use it to pay the bill?

———————●———————

No one likes wasting time in line at the checkout, and the **Lowe's** home improvement chain knows it. They make a written promise: Lowe's will open another register anytime there are three or more customers waiting in line to pay.

———————●———————

How many times have you thought you could do a better job than that slow-moving cashier? Now, you can prove it. **Winn-Dixie** is testing an automated checkout system known as CheckRobot in several areas, including Charlotte, North Carolina. Scan your own groceries, swipe your card, and sign the receipt on the way out the door. And, when you need groceries, you can be sure Winn-Dixie is open, 24 hours a day.

———————●———————

The nation's largest tax preparation firm **H&R Block, Inc.** is always coming up with ways to bring customers back. Now, they offer re-fund-anticipation loans, so clients can receive their refunds within 48 hours, instead of waiting for the IRS to refund the money. It's a fee-based convenience, but it works.

───────●───────

Going to a stand-alone store to prepare your taxes too inconvenient? Try **Tax One,** which serves Ogden, Utah, by opening temporary offices at tax time in grocery stores.

───────●───────

Walk into your typical full-service broker-age, and if your broker isn't available, most likely neither is help with your account. Discount broker **Charles Schwab,** on the other hand, welcomes walk-ins. Schwab employees are cross-trained and have access to all accounts, so virtually any branch office employee will be able to assist you.

───────●───────

Some budget-conscious businesses don't accept the **American Express** card because of its higher merchant fees, so the company supplies its cardholders with checks for when the credit card cannot be used. Unlike many credit card checks, there are no transaction fees and checks may be written for any purpose, including balance transfers, taxes, major purchases, vacations, etc., as long as they are for more than $100. And, because the checks are based on cardholders' Optima account, balances may be paid over time rather than in full at the end of the month.

───────●───────

The **Prime Time Video** rental chain knows that customers like to rent more than one video at a time but are often constrained by the time they need to watch them. To clear this hurdle,

If our customer wants to use the American Express card at a hot dog stand, we want to be there.

—AMERICAN EXPRESS'S
KENNETH CHENAULT IN
CUSTOMER SERVICE

and encourage multiple rentals, the chain offers different return dates on different movies. New releases are 24 hours, recent releases can be held for 48 hours, and older movie rentals are good for 72 hours, all at the same charge.

———————⊛———————

Hollywood Video, the nation's second-largest video store chain, is eliminating the run on new movies by ordering them under a revenue-sharing arrangement rather than as an outright purchase. By essentially leasing movies for $8 to $12 per copy plus half the movie's rental revenue, the chain avoids paying the up-front purchase prices of about $70 and can afford to stock many more copies. The savings are so great that the chain now rents any video in the store for a full five days for just 25¢ more than the usual rental fee.

———————⊛———————

Our local **Cattails** boutique sells specialty women's clothing and accessories from the very casual to the semi-formal. Occasionally, items arrive from the manufacturer in unfinished lengths in order to be custom-fit to the purchaser. How long before they will be ready? Thirty minutes! Cattails teamed up with a nearby seamstress to speed minor alterations, and it's a free service.

———————⊛———————

Can't get to a theater to see the plays you love? **Globalstage** will bring the theater to you. The company sells subscription-based series of live plays, including world-premiers as well as the classics such as *Cyrano*, on video. Each is professionally filmed by the BBC and includes behind-the-scenes segments and historical references. The "season" currently includes six plays, arriving one every three months.

Convenience is so important to customers these days, it often becomes the basis for whole new businesses. Richmond, Virginia–based **RENT A MOM** was founded on that principle. Customers can arrange for any domestic service they need, such as cooking, cleaning, shopping, and other errands; pet and baby sitting; and many other services that can otherwise chip away at already limited evening and weekend hours. And, customers purchase the service as often as they want, even if it's just once. Rent A Mom gives customers what they really want—a break.

Gift certificates for individual visits from **Merry Maids** serve a similar purpose. Just use one when you need extra help.

Audible Web (www.audible.com) kicked off its business by making the daily *Wall Street Journal* available for those who simply don't have the time to read it themselves. Subscribers pay $6.95 per month to download a 30-minute abridged audio version of the *Wall Street Journal* from Audible Web's site online and use a $199 portable audio player to listen to the paper in the shower, while driving, or wherever.

Canada's **BMW Financial Services** makes it simple for lease customers to come back for more with its BMW Pre-Approval Card. Three months before their current lease ends, customers in good standing are sent the card, which entitles them to walk into any Canadian BMW dealership and sign up for a new car without any additional credit approvals. There are no monthly payment limitations and all BMW models are included.

─────── ◈ ───────

Wonder where that car goes when the lease is up? Could be **Circuit City's** super-sized Car-Max chain. CarMax is all about ease: Its automobiles are stickered at the lowest price; there is plenty of choice—dealers have over 1,400 used vehicles of various makes and models plus new cars; online previewing is available; and, used cars carry the "Worry-Free Limited 30-Day Warranty and a 5-day/250 mile Money-Back Guarantee."

─────── ◈ ───────

Mattel, Inc. subsidiary Fisher-Price encourages toy-lovers to choose its products before they ever get to the toy store. The company's Web site includes a Personal Shopper that searches by criteria such as age, price, category of toy, or special occasion. Once the perfect toy is located, visit the directory of stores carrying the product to locate the one nearby.

─────── ◈ ───────

Don't close; automate. **Granite Rock Company** supplies paving and concrete products for construction projects in California, some of which run round the clock until the job is done. To meet their customers' demand for raw materials 24 hours a day, the company unveiled GraniteXpress, an automatic loading system that is activated by an ATM-type card. Drivers swipe the card, select the product, and their trucks are automatically loaded.

─────── ◈ ───────

The best for last: Virginia's **Swampbilly Bait Company** is operating "the industry's only state-of-the-art 24-hour live bait vending machine." Located in four strategic locations at grocery stores, marinas, and campgrounds, the machines offer customers six appetizing baits, including chicken necks that come with string for crabbing and that old standby, the night-crawler. The Vending Concepts, Inc., machines are available 24/7, a real boon for early-rising fishermen.

9

GO TO YOUR CUSTOMERS

This book is predicated on the belief that companies should want to keep customers coming back. But, that doesn't necessarily mean customers should actually come to you at all. Maybe the best way to keep customers coming back is to go to them.

There are two great reasons to go to your customers:

First, they need to know when it's time to do business with you. There is nothing wrong with telling your customers when it's time to buy more of your products and services. In fact, reminders are often perceived as a valuable service for busy people who have a hard time keeping track of details such as checkups and replacements. Reminders are common tools among doctors and magazine publishers, but with a little imagination many businesses can adopt this technique.

Second, whenever possible, bring your goods and services to the customer. House calls are rare in the medical profession nowadays, but there is a growing trend that may speed their return. More and more businesses are realizing that the ultimate service for customers is to have products or services delivered to their point of use.

NOTIFY WHEN IT'S TIME TO BUY

On the one-year anniversary of new Explorer purchases, **Ford Motor Company** sends a personalized letter to the buyer along with a $500 cash bonus toward the purchase or lease of a new Explorer. The letter highlights the upgraded features of the new model and advises the location of the nearest Ford dealer, even if that is not where the original model was purchased. Finally, they offer a low-interest financing arrangement through Ford Credit for qualified buyers.

———— • ————

The **Country Christmas Tree Farm** in Sebastopol, California, uses a simple technique to thank its customers for their business and remind them to visit again at the same time. The farm waits until Thanksgiving before sending "thank you for your business" postcards to everyone who purchased a tree the previous year. Just in case you don't get the hint, the postcard includes a road map to the farm.

———— • ————

DimeLine is another single call-based long-distance provider that needs to stand out from the crowd. It puts a spin on the ubiquitous refrigerator magnet by sending customers batches of free reminder stickers in various sizes and suggesting that they be stuck directly on telephones and directories. No need to remember that number; it's there when you need it.

———— • ————

At renewal time, *Esquire* magazine sends a notice that differentiates itself in many ways. First, the message is personalized—it mentions the subscriber's full name no less than eight times on one page. Second, it thanks the reader for his or her loyalty. Third, in addition to offering the now standard discount from cover price, the letter promises a free, surprise gift.

———— • ————

Ever wonder what happens to all those warranty cards manufacturers receive? **Optiva,** maker of the Sonicare-brand specialty toothbrush, puts its warranty cards to work to generate repeat business for the replacement brush heads Sonicare owners need. In less than 60 days from receipt of Sonicare warranty cards, the company sends a "$5 off your next brush head purchase" coupon to the new owner. The card offers the option of purchasing the brush head and mailing in the card for a rebate or buying the brush head via a toll-free number for instant savings.

———— • ————

Whether you've bought your car there or only go there for service, Ford dealer **Williamsburg Motors** estimates the miles you'll drive and sends a personalized reminder notice when it's time for service based on the manufacturer's recommended maintenance schedule. They even include an appointment date for you to keep or reschedule and several relevant service coupons.

———— • ————

Quick oil change artists **SpeeDee Oil Change & Tune Up** make customers aware of when to schedule their next service appointment by sticking the information right on their car's windshield. For those who peel that sticker off, SpeeDee also mails reminder postcards that offer discounts on targeted services.

———— • ————

Blue Cross & Blue Shield of Massachusetts created a greeting card reminder program for members who become parents. Since members have only 30 days to add their newborn to their

---

Five Rules for Customer Communiqués

1. Make it fast: No one has time to waste.

2. Personalize the message: You know their names, use them.

3. Lead with WIIFM: Explain "what's in it for me," up front.

4. Say thank you: Express appreciation for past business *and* the time they just spent.

5. Let them respond: Make sure they can easily contact you.

The golden rule for every businessman is this: Put yourself in your customer's place.

—ORISON SWETT MARDEN,
FOUNDER OF
SUCCESS MAGAZINE

healthcare plan, the first card in the series is a message of congratulations that includes an immunization card and a reminder to add their newborn to their policy. The second card is sent on the baby's first birthday, just to be nice.

———————— ✦ ————————

Williamsburg, Virginia–based dentist **Bruce DeGinder** has a smart, simple way to keep customers coming back. He sets up the next appointment before they leave the last as part of his Prevention Recall Program. Even if that appointment is simply for the now standard semi-annual cleaning and is six months away, the appointment is made and in the computer. The office always sends a reminder postcard the week before an appointment and makes a reminder call to clients the day before an appointment, so this program works even for those who do not keep a calendar.

———————— ✦ ————————

Intuit, Inc., the largest personal finance software company, has a very profitable sideline in the checks, forms, and other supplies designed to be used with its QuickBooks and Quicken packages. They keep printing customers coming back with a personalized reminder letter that is timed according to usage patterns. Moreover, Intuit offers an additional incentive in the form of a 20% discount.

Want to know where your order is? Intuit has a new "Order Status Notification" service. Provide them with an e-mail address or fax number, and you are notified when the order is entered into the Intuit system and again when it ships—this time with the shipper's tracking number.

———————— ✦ ————————

Death, taxes, and now, the latest versions of tax preparation software are inevitable. **Block**

Financial Corporation's Kiplinger TaxCut software makes sure it continues to be the program of choice among its customers with personalized reminder letters mailed long before the new tax season begins. The subsidiary of H&R Block sends along an order form and a nice bundle of extras, which in 1998 included free clip art software and a bonus game.

———— ● ————

The **Clorox Company's** Brita Water Filtration Systems keeping customers coming back with a product filter that must be replaced every 14 to 60 days, depending on usage. Brita notifies when it is time to buy with its "Brita Filter Change Calendar," printed on a sticker that can be placed on the pitcher itself or the fridge door. They also offer a $2 mail-in rebate to encourage the first filter replacement purchase.

———— ● ————

Once a week, registered customers get an e-mail from **Ukrop's Super Markets.** A one pager, it tells about new merchandise in the store and highlights some of the current special offers. In the letter is a hot link; click on it and off you go to the chain's Web site and this week's exclusive online coupons, all ready for selection and printing.

———— ● ————

Renewals are extremely important at **Nutrition Action Healthletter,** a monthly publication of the Center for Science in the Public Interest. (CSPI is a nonprofit organization dedicated to safeguarding the public health through truth in labeling, advertising, and information.) It sustains itself almost entirely on revenues from the newsletter's one million subscribers. So, it begins notifying six months before its customers' subscriptions lapse with an "Early-Bird" 15% discount and a free bonus issue offer. And, the publication makes sure you know that it's a one-time offer and follow-up incentives to renew will not be as attractive.

———————— • ————————

Colonial Williamsburg (CW) prices its guest passes to the 173-acre living history museum so that the high-end, one-year Patriot's Pass is the most attractive option for those who want full access to the facilities. CW is also diligent about getting them renewed: Patriot's Pass owners receive personalized letters advising that their passes are about to expire and invit-ing them to renew by phone or mail—a boon for out-of-towners, who previously needed to renew in person, and a revenue builder for CW. Finally, the historic institution keeps its pass holders appraised of seasonal events with regular mailings of calendars. The Spring 1999 mailing starts, "You probably don't know about our spring events . . . But you've already bought a ticket for them."

———————— • ————————

Largo, Florida–based **Eckerd Corporation** makes sure its prescription drug clientele knows what time it is with a personalized letter alerting when it's time for a refill. It also ex-tends the service to seasonal drugs; as spring nears, Eckerd reminds clients to start thinking about their allergy medications.

———————— • ————————

There's nothing like being a flea in spring-time and **PETsMART** knows it. The chain noti-fies its customers that it's time to buy pet pest prevention products with its "Flea Free Fri-days." Stop in at the VetSmart department and get your best friend a free look-see. They'll "check your Pet for fleas, flea dirt, broken skin and prescribe the best product for Flea preven-tion and control."

We know a big fan of Northeast New Jersey's **Bernini's,** a clothing store whose salespeople know enough about the clients to call them when new merchandise they would like arrives and to check on how that new suit looks.

———— ● ————

Here's a simple idea: Why not let one customer notify another when its time to buy? **Dillard's Inc.** placed a stack of "Just A Hint" cards, printed with the store's name and location, at every cash register. Customers choose an item in the store that they would like to receive as a gift, write it on the card, and as Dillard's suggests, "tuck the card under a pillow, by a toothbrush, or in a shoe to let a loved one know." Where are you going to go to fulfill that wish?

———— ● ————

Each year, the Williamsburg Folk Art Show returns to the College of William & Mary and each year, the management team at **Virginia Craft Festivals** offers a little extra to ensure the return of the regulars. About a month ahead of the show, postcards are mailed to last year's attendees advising them of the date of this year's show. They double as a coupon for $1 off the $5 admission price, an added incentive to return. How do they get the names? The previous year's visitors filled out entry forms for door prizes.

———— ● ————

The Peppers and Rogers Group's free weekly e-letter *Inside 1to1* alerted us to Belgium's **Spector Photo Group,** a retail film developer, which tracks its clients' purchases and preferences at the point of sale. Using that information and a short survey for first-time customers, Spector employees can not only identify customers when they pop in, they can also remind them

Who Are Your Customers?

Everybody's got customers, no matter where in the organization they work. There are external customers—the folks who buy products and services from your company. And, there are internal customers—the folks inside your company who depend on your work to complete theirs. If you can't keep both of them coming back, you will soon be out of work.

Why Start a Newsletter?

- To introduce employees to customers
- To give an added-value bonus
- To introduce new products and services
- To celebrate successes (yours and your customers)
- To say thanks

on the spot when additional services, such as a camera battery change, might be needed.

———— • ————

And speaking of e-letters (newsletters delivered via e-mail) . . . they are a great way to give your customers valuable information and stay in touch at the same time. **The Peppers and Rogers Group** offers case studies, relevant news, and info on their fast-growing company in their weekly *Inside 1to1* to anyone who requests a subscription at the Web site, www.1to1.com (Last time we heard that was over 30,000 people.)

———— • ————

Here at **The Business Reader,** we publish a free monthly e-letter called *The Business Reader Review* that combs each month's new business books for 10 to 20 of the best and offers a capsule review of each. Customers appreciate knowing what's new on the bookshelf and because there is no advertising or sales-hype allowed, know that the information is honestly offered. Be happy to give it to you; just e-mail bizbooks@gte.net

———— • ————

Artists and art dealers have going to their customers down to a science with the seemingly endless rounds of arts and craft shows staged around the country. Buy a piece of handmade furniture from **Windsors by Bill Wallick,** a furniture craftsman from Wrightsville, Pennsylvania, and Bill makes sure you know when he is nearby. To be certain that the traditional crafts shows in which he exhibits are well populated with past customers, Wallick sends special invitations. One month prior to the Designer Craftsmen Show of Philadelphia, his clients received a glossy brochure featuring his work and free admission for two to the show, a $20 value.

———— ◉ ————

Cleveland, Ohio–based art gallery **The Verne Collection** keeps in touch with its out-of-town collectors of Japanese art in the same way. To reach the Mid-Atlantic region, gallery owner Michael Verne attends the Annual Washington International Print Fair. To make sure his customers do too, a personalized letter advises them that their names will be on the Guest List at the door, saving the $6 per person admission fee.

———— ◉ ————

Norwalk, Connecticut–based **1-800 BIRTH-DAY** has built a complete business around the idea of notifying when it's time to buy. Customers use the Birthday Bank to provide the company with the names and birthdays of friends and family. At a suitable interval before the date, they are reminded by e-mail, postal mail, or telephone. As for the gifts themselves, simply choose from various goodies in the company's catalog or on its Web site (www.1-800birthday.com).

———— ◉ ————

The Gap, Inc.'s online store offers its customers a personal electronic shopping organizer. Among other things, it will store the names and addresses of 10 friends and relatives and 50 important dates associated with them. Once entered, it sends you an e-mail reminder two weeks ahead of every one of the 50 entered dates.

———— ◉ ————

Customers usually call North Carolina–based **Replacements, Ltd.,** to find that discontinued piece of china, crystal, or silverware. But, who knows how many sales the company missed because customers did not know that a

There are no traffic
jams when you go the
extra mile.

—UNKNOWN

hard-to-find piece of this or that pattern came into stock? Problem solved: the company now keeps customers informed economically via e-mail. Just register for the patterns you're interested in online and Replacements will tell you what they've found on a regular basis.

BRING IT TO THE CUSTOMER

Once you have gone to your customers to notify them it's time to buy, don't stop. Bring the goods and services they want right to their door. **General Motor's** luxury car division Cadillac is trying exactly that with its new program called "Anytime, Anywhere." Now in the pilot stage, Cadillac dealers will deliver a new car to any location the customer stipulates. The dealer will also meet customers away from the dealership with lease or purchase agreements or to make an instant offer on any trade-ins. If buyers are uncertain whether Cadillac is their car of choice, the dealer will deliver a car to any customer location for a free two-day test drive. After an agreement is reached, the new car will be delivered and the trade-in taken away at any time and any location the customer requests.

———— • ————

Aspen, Colorado's **Little Nell Hotel** doesn't wait for its guest to arrive to begin making them comfortable. It calls each visitor prior to arrival to answer questions about the area and the hotel, make plans for dinners and airport transfers, and suggest and arrange recreational activities.

———— • ————

If you actually mail orders to mail-orders, you never really know that everything is proceeding apace. Except at **Fingerhut Companies,**

Inc. Not only do you get your goods delivered to your door; you also get a courtesy call when the order is received, confirming it and advising when you can expect to receive it.

————————— ✦ —————————

FDX Corporation's FedEx delivery service will tell your customers when their package is on its way. Process your packages using the company's online software, supply your customer's e-mail address, and FedEx will e-mail them when to expect the package.

————————— ✦ —————————

Don't have a product to deliver? Take a lesson from our local realtor **Cale & Company,** which regularly sends useful information to customers and prospects. For example, a pre-printed postcard that simply reminds them of the impending time change: "Just a reminder to Spring Forward on April 5, 1998!" A nice way to put your company name in front of your customers without a full-blown sales pitch.

————————— ✦ —————————

College & University Computers (CUC) keeps its name in front of its customers by sending its "Technology Update" newsletter. In addition to informative articles and industry news, it includes details on upcoming sales, services offered, coupons, and highlights about the company. A recent issue gave customers details on how to sign up for automatic e-mail notification of unadvertised clearance and discontinued items, another service we like.

————————— ✦ —————————

Like many companies, Washington-based **Seattle Filmworks, Inc.** is using the Internet to reach its customers. Send in a roll of film from anywhere in the world, and the $100 million photo finisher will digitize the film and send it

> In every instance, we found that the best-run companies stay as close to their customers as humanly possible.
>
> —Tom Peters

back on disk or via the Internet. They'll also make a personal screen saver for your computer from your film. This is from the same company that built its business by sending consumers free rolls of film to introduce them to its service.

———— • ————

Third largest chain in the office supply superstore category, Ohio-based **OfficeMax, Inc.,** saves its customers time as well as money. Meet the minimum order limit at your local store and it delivers for free the next business day.

———— • ————

In 1984, **1-800-Flowers, Inc.** put together BloomNet, a network of 2,500 partner florists, to create same-day delivery of flowers, wherever you want them to go. In 1995, the world's largest florist added its own Web site to the mix—eliminating the phone call and adding the ability to actually see the flowers you are buying.

———— • ————

Making sure customers can come back to you via whatever route they choose is emerging as an important retention strategy. The **Charles Schwab Corporation** provides every conceivable avenue: you can purchase stocks in person at their offices; use the automated phone system; call a real, live human; or buy online. All are linked through the company's computer network, and you decide which you prefer.

———— • ————

Swedish carmaker **Volvo Svenska Bil** went into the insurance business on its home soil so it could regularly go to its customers. Customer service expert Karl Albrecht said it all in his *Quality Digest* column: "If a car buyer disappears into customerland after leaving the dealership, the company has to wait (or pay) for the customer to show up again. With a continuity product such as insurance, the continuing contact provides opportunities to build preference and strengthen the buyer-seller relationship."

———————•———————

Richmond, Virginia's Scott Overman found a great way to keep busy people coming back to **Creative Enterprise,** his car detailing service—he goes to them. For a rate of $20 to $100 depending on the depth of the service and the size of the vehicle, Overman shows up at any area home or business with all the necessary equipment, including 300 gallons of water and a generator to run a vacuum and power washer.

———————•———————

Our local **Wiz Auto Wash** also offers custom auto detailing and brushless car washes. To set itself apart from the competition and make it easy for customers to keep coming back, Wiz offers a pickup and delivery service from its clients' homes or offices.

———————•———————

Maybe **Mail Boxes Etc.** (MBE) can't come all the way to your door, but it has teamed up with USA Technologies to create MBE Business Express, a chain of unmanned kiosks that provide business services in hotels including Marriott and Best Westerns. They can also be found in grocery stores, convenience marts, and convention centers. The kiosks operate 24 hours a day and are activated with a credit card. Customers get access to a personal computer and the Internet along with a laser printer, fax, copier, and laptop hookup.

———————•———————

From the do-I-really-want-these-guys-at-my-door department, East Meredith, New York–based **Catskill Casket Co.** has revolutionized their business by selling direct to the consumer

> **Customers will buy more if you meet them where they want to do business. Otherwise, they will buy less.**
>
> —LAWRENCE FRIEDMAN AND TIMOTHY FUREY IN *THE CHANNEL ADVANTAGE*

in a dealership-based industry. Prices are much lower—they cut out the huge funeral home mark-up—and the company ships "your" casket overnight directly to the funeral home of your choice.

————————— ◉ —————————

Leading microprocessor maker **Intel Corporation** reached out to its ultimate customer, the end-user, with its highly successful "Intel Inside" brand-building campaign. The strategy created a brand name in the minds of PC buyers, who up until that point had little idea what was in that box on their desks. Even better, Intel shared the stage with the products that incorporate their chips and thus, shared the costs of marketing and advertising, too.

————————— ◉ —————————

Yes, Virginia, they still make house calls. San Diego **HotelDocs** make "house calls" to sick travelers in their hotel rooms. The service is available in over 250 U.S. cities and draws from a network over 2,500 practicing physicians, dentists, chiropractors, and even, psychiatrists. Just call 800-HOTEL-DR.

————————— ◉ —————————

Don't forget the Internet! Book industry revolutionary **Amazon.com** is well known and well rewarded for bringing the bookstore to the customer. The first company to put a bookstore online in a big way, Amazon is the market leader. And, really, unless you want a cup of coffee, you never have to go to a bookstore again.

————————— ◉ —————————

Drugstore.com took a similar tack with the local drugstore. In addition to all the usual products, customers can fill or refill their prescriptions from their desks and the orders are sent directly to their homes. The company offers all the services of the druggist and will even call your doctor at your request. In addition, you can e-mail or call the staff pharmacists with any questions. It's an idea so good that Amazon.com recently bought the company.

————— • —————

Hesitant to buy heavy furniture from direct marketers? Look for the "HH" symbol in the **Horchow Home Collection** catalog. Items so designated include unpacking and arranging your purchase in your home at no additional charge. They'll even clean up and cart away packing materials when they're through.

————— • —————

United Parcel Service (UPS) makes going to its customers for a scheduled daily pickup standard procedure. But, just in case you have an additional air shipment that must be on its way, it also offers On Call Air Pickup service. UPS daily pickup accounts may either call a toll-free number or go online to arrange for a post-pickup pickup at no extra charge.

————— • —————

The **City of Richmond, Virginia,** encourages streetwalkers. Well, not exactly. To encourage tourism, Richmond has sent a small army of ambassadors into the downtown streets. The ambassadors help keep the city clean, safe, and—most of all—are available to help or provide information to visitors. Similar to a hotel's concierge and dressed to attract attention, they actively look for people who need help. They carry maps to assist with directions and make suggestions on where to eat, shop, or visit. They will also carry radios and can alert the police in case of any unusual or unlawful activity. Showing true southern hospitality, Richmond is not only inviting people to visit, it is going out to meet them.

————— • —————

To keep customers coming back you have to enable them to reach your company through any sales channel they wish— through the Internet, over the phone, going to a store, or talking to a sales representative. This is the secret of fast-growth companies like Dell and Schwab: They integrate sales channels to make it easy for customers to shop and buy. The results go straight to their bottom line: Increased customer loyalty, lower costs of sales, and accelerated revenue growth.

—Timothy Furey,
CEO of Oxford Associates

Don't have time to get to a spa? **BASU** will send it to you. Its Spa of the Month Club sends a new pampering package each month. The first month is the most expensive at $30 and includes three products especially suited to making the home feel like a spa, along with a scented candle and potpourri to set the mood. Subsequent months bring packaged spa treatments including luxurious mud facials and clay masks right to the customer's home for about $9 each.

———————●———————

Want voice lessons from Sherman Oaks, California–based instructor Jeffrey Allen, but you live in New York? No problem. The **Jeffrey Allen Virtual Voice Studio** is equipped for videoconferencing technology, so its owner will be happy to come to you, when and where you want to take a lesson.

———————●———————

Remember going to the car dealership and poring over the options packages? Forget it. Stop in at the **Bayerische Motoren Werke AG** Web site, and you can put the BMW of your dreams together. Not only can you specify the exact car you want; you can get a delivery date, and pay for it!

———————●———————

Remember going to the furniture store for your mattress? Forget it. Shop online at Long Island City, New York's **Dial A Mattress** and you can do everything except bounce. Pick the style you like best or let the company recommend a mattress for you. Either way, within 24 hours, your mattress is at your door.

———————●———————

Over the decades, a field trip to **Colonial Williamsburg** (CW) has become a standard experience for students throughout the Mid-

Atlantic region. Now, CW is extending its reach to those unable to visit in person. Satellite broadcasting and a full-equipped TV studio enable the foundation to produce low-cost electronic field trips. School systems around the country purchase the live, interactive broadcasts, so schoolchildren can learn eighteenth century American history first-hand without ever leaving their classrooms.

———●———

The **Wholesale Rug Outlet** (WRO) in Lancaster, Pennsylvania, will bring its huge selection of Oriental and tribal rugs to your home—anywhere. Describe the type of rug you are looking for, and WRO will gladly use their digital camera to photograph a selection of choices and e-mail them to your desk. See one you like? Order via phone or e-mail and it's on its way.

———●———

Our local rug store **Oriental Textile Arts** isn't shy about going to its customers either. They are happy to visit your home, give advice on selecting the appropriate rugs, and bring their recommendations back to your home, so you can live with them for awhile before you make the purchase decision. No extra charge.

———●———

Pennzoil-Quaker State's Q-Lube Marine Services is a new franchise that fills a niche in the boating world. Q-Lube charges a flat fee for a standard package of boat maintenance services, including an oil and filter change, topping off fluids, cleaning, and parts inspection. But, the best part is that Q-Lube goes to your boat. They bring their equipment, expertise, and mechanics to a dock, marina, or even your driveway.

———●———

Need some quick advice from a consultant? Call Ernie. Ernie is **Ernst & Young International's** online consulting service for companies that just need a little help here and there. Companies subscribe to Ernie, paying fees based on their number of users. In return, they get electronic access to the New York City–based consulting firm's database and staff. Ask your questions, and Ernst & Young will e-mail responses.

———— • ————

The **Tom Jones Company** of Richmond, Virginia, values their customers' business as well as their time. The company's tailors bring both ready-made and custom-fitted men's clothing—including shirts, suits, ties, and even shoes—to your office. They collect all the information they need beforehand, so there is no need to review problem areas, price ranges, or even favored styles and labels. Measurements are taken, merchandise presented, choices made, and away they go.

———— • ————

Fort Myers, Florida–based **Fish Master** cuts a huge chunk out of the up to 14-day journey "fresh" fish takes to get to your local market. Customers can phone or e-mail the company to place their orders for fresh grouper, snapper, mackerel, and shrimp. Once caught on one of Fish Master's two weekly trips into the Gulf, your order is shipped overnight directly to your door.

———— • ————

Daytona Beach–based **John Crane Belfab** can't send its manufacturing employees to work at its customers' plants, but the maker of welded seals and bellows can sure make them feel that way. The company dedicates space on its flexible shop floor to its major customers. It paints the walls in those areas with the customer's company colors and logos, and Belfab employees know the area by the customer's names—sometimes they even answer the phone that way.

——————— ● ———————

Customers still have to take their cars to the gas pump, but two **Chevron** stations in Antioch, California, are making sure they don't have to go any further. While customers pump gas at the station, they can also order a car wash, food and drink, and even a long-distance phone card from the touch screen on the pump. A swipe of the credit card and the station clerks deliver the goods to the car.

10

GIVE CUSTOMERS WHAT THEY WANT

The days of Henry Ford offering customers the Model T "in any color they want, as long as it's black" are long gone. Today, if companies want to earn the business of loyal customers, they need to find out what their customers want and give it to them.

There are three principles for giving customers what they want:

1. *Listen to their desires.* The importance of listening to customers is often forgotten in a fast-paced environment. Listening can be accomplished on a large or small scale; it can be formal or informal. The important thing is that information gleaned be treated as a valuable commodity that will shape the course of the organization.

2. *Create the services and products they demand.* Listening to customers is a waste of time for you and your customers unless you act. Once you identify customer desires, it's time to build them what they want.

3. *Personalize it for each individual customer.* Almost anything from audio CDs to jeans can be "mass customized" today. Mass customization acknowledges that all consumers are not alike

and allows companies to cater to the specific needs of all of its customers at prices that reflect mass production techniques. So, learn how to customize and start dealing with large numbers of customers on an individualized basis.

LISTEN TO THE VOICE OF THE CUSTOMER

The first computer giant **IBM** lost its way for a few years but is quickly returning to a position of great power. One way it accomplished its turnaround was by listening to its customers. Today, groups of 20 customers known as "Customer Advisory Councils" meet regularly with Big Blue. Their input helps shape IBM's current product lines and future plans.

The computer maker also taps into customer knowledge on the telephone. Employees in the manufacturing arena are given temporary three-month assignments during which they phone recent buyers. Customers are not only asked what they like about their new purchase, but more importantly, what they don't like.

———— ● ————

Apple Computer listens through its Customer Quality Feedback (CQF) program. The company field tests its new products by sending them to groups of customers gathered in a Web-based application process. In return, the customers send the company their opinions and feedback.

———— ● ————

Merry Maids isn't the least expensive cleaning service available, but it makes a science out of listening to its customers. Sign up for the service and the franchise owner or manager spends a good deal of time on your premises learning to

Go talk to customers, and talk to customers you didn't get.

—Scott Cook, CEO of Intuit, Inc. in *Sam's Club Source* magazine what you want cleaned and how you want it cleaned. The results of this survey are transformed into a computer printout that the regular cleaning team uses to direct its work.

————— ● —————

Pleasanton, California–based **Peoplesoft, Inc.** uses a game on its Web site to induce customers to share their preferences. The site offers "PeopleDollars" play money with which customers can "buy" their favorites from lists of possible new features on the company's corporate management software.

————— ● —————

Philadelphia-based **Rosenbluth International** became the third-largest U.S. travel agency by listening to and learning from its customers. It created a fee-based service that pays for itself because it cuts its clients' overall travel expenses by searching out the best value for their dollars. It even combines the overall volume of its client base to negotiate lower airfares on heavily traveled routes.

Rosenbluth goes so far as to hold joint strategy sessions with its customers, creating multi-year plans that make sure the agency delivers the most benefit possible. "From these sessions, we gain a clear understanding of where each of our clients is headed, so we can ensure that we have the right resources to be where they need us in the future," explains CEO Hal Rosenbluth in *Good Company*.

————— ● —————

Just when you've decided that complaining is a waste of time, **General Motors Corporation's** Delphi Energy & Engine Management Systems plant comes along. The Grand Rapids, Michigan, plant calculates the top five customer complaints from each previous year and works to eliminate them in the current year.

> When a customer offers you criticism or advice, take it. Be grateful for it. Take notes. Thank the customer. Ask for more.
>
> —**Darby Checketts** in *Customer Astonishment*

> We view a customer who is complaining as a real blessing in disguise. He or she is someone we can resell.
>
> —LOUIS CARBONE

———— ● ————

Columbus, Ohio–based process-control equipment maker **ABB Industrial Systems** quit measuring customer satisfaction to pay more attention to dissatisfaction. The company's customer complaint resolution process encourages complaints, determines their causes, and takes action to make sure they are eliminated.

———— ● ————

Worcester, Massachusetts's **Fallon Clinic** monitored its customer complaints and found that many centered around one department's doctors. It quickly used training to improve the docs' interpersonal skills and complaints dropped by nearly two-thirds.

———— ● ————

Companies that don't listen to customers—especially complaining ones—are asking for trouble. Maybe the complainer will log onto **Service Intelligence, Inc.'s** Web site (www.serviceintelligence.com) and blast away. Or, maybe they will simply create their own site to disparage your company throughout the cyberworld. Or, maybe they'll take a lesson from the irate Starbuck's customer who went public with his complaint in a $10,000, full-page ad in the *Wall Street Journal*.

———— ● ————

Internet service provider **Erol's Internet, Inc.** uses a combination of tech support and its very best customer service reps to try to convince dissatisfied customers to give the company another try. CEO Orhan Onaran told *WebWeek*, ". . . if a person is frustrated due to a technical problem, a technical support person remains on standby to help, so we don't lose anyone for that reason." The result has been an 81% retention rate on cancellation calls.

Due to scandals and the ensuing drop in prize money, the **State of Texas** Lottery is one of the few that suffered sales losses—up to $10 million per week in 1996 and 1997. To revitalize the program, the state studied exactly how the winners spent their newfound wealth. Finding that shiny new trucks were high on their priority lists, Texas created an instant lottery that pays off in limited-edition pickup trucks.

Cypress, California–based **PacifiCare** calculated its cost of finding a new member as three times that of keeping an existing one. With that in mind, the HMO reached out to customers who left the organization to find out why. It then attacked those reasons, such as incomplete program descriptions by sales reps, lack of chiropractor services, impersonal service, unwieldy referral processes, and prescription drug limitations, to build its retention percentage.

British Airways, Plc. created CARESS (Customer Analysis & Retention System) after realizing that repeat sales drop off by 60% if a customer's complaint is not quickly resolved. The new system puts complaints through a 13-step process—but only involves the customer in the 10th step. It works, too: *Industry-Week* reported that a 12-week complaint backlog was eliminated and that 80% of the complaining customers indicated they would fly the carrier again.

Tax accounting firm **Eggleston Smith P.C.** has a memorable, and tasty, way of asking for their clients' feedback. After a consultation, clients receive a card in the mail thanking

One who never asks either knows everything or nothing.

—Malcolm Forbes

Most large businesses lose and must replace half of their customers every year, according to Frederick Reichheld in The Loyalty Effect.

them for their business and mentioning the company's goal: "100% client satisfaction." It asks them to take a survey about their experience and as a small token, includes fortune cookies with messages, such as "We count it our good fortune to have you as our client."

———————————●———————————

Chicago-based **Wilson Sporting Goods Company** owns around 50% of the domestic market for tennis rackets. How did it build its share? By watching and listening to customers in sporting goods stores, according to CEO Jim Baugh. He explained to *IndustryWeek* magazine: "If you just sit back and look at numbers and reports, you don't feel the emotion of the purchase—what turns customers on and motivates them to think about your product."

———————————●———————————

Redmond, Washington–based emergency medical equipment maker **Physio-Control** uses focus groups and conferences to collect the customer suggestions, opinions, and needs it uses to inform the early stages of the product design process. The company's free customer training, already given to over 20,000 nurses, paramedics, and other emergency care personnel, is also mined for improvement ideas.

———————————●———————————

Wooster, Ohio–based **Seaman Corporation** weaved its way out of a period of flat sales by paying closer attention to customers. The company jet was dispatched to bring them to the polymer-coated fabrics maker for one-day learning sessions aimed at connecting Seaman's capabilities with customer needs. "We have invited 40 to 50 customers here," said CEO Richard Seaman. "Previously, only 4 to 5 visited in a year." Among the results: a 58% sales jump.

———— ● ————

Brazil's **Banco Bradesco** uses customers to help drive its new product development process. For example, a request from a small business customer to help manage cash flow resulted in a software program that thousands of its customers now use. Another request yielded an ATM-type card that corporate customers' employees use to draw their salaries.

———— ● ————

WinterSilks, a direct marketer of silk clothing and accessories, set up a toll-free line so customers could easily express their opinions about the firm's products and services. It uses this input to improve their policies. For example, when customers complained about shipping fees based on total dollar amount of the purchase, the company began to charge by weight. The company also added more detail to item descriptions as well as additional size ranges based on customer requests.

———— ● ————

When customers take the time to tell you what they think, thank them. Asheville, North Carolina's famous **Grove Park Inn and Country Club** responded to a Guest Comment request card praising an employee with a personal thank-you letter from the Executive Assistant Manager. The letter informed the customer that the employee would receive a Notice of Commendation as a result of his praise and expressed the hope that the customer would return soon.

———— ● ————

The Walt Disney Company also uses questionnaires to evaluate the hospitality provided at the Disneyland Hotel from its guests' perspectives. To encourage guests to take the time to complete the questionnaire, Disneyland

> If you want to have more successful relationships with your customers, your family, and your friends, look at things from the other person's perspective.
>
> —DALE CARNEGIE

Get a customer to in-
vest time teaching a
business what he or
she needs, and that
customer will be less
likely to go else-
where. The marketer
wins loyalty. The cus-
tomer wins individu-
alized service.

—MARTHA ROGERS IN
INSIDE 1TO1

sends it along with a thank-you letter for
choosing the Disneyland Hotel in Anaheim
and a raffle ticket. Return the questionnaire and
ticket within two weeks and you are entered in
the "Ears to You" contest. Winners receive a
two-night stay for four, breakfast, and passes for
free. Disney gets important feedback.

———————— ● ————————

Talk about listening to the customer! **General Motors Corporation's** OnStar option uses
global positioning and cellular communications networks to stay in touch with their cars
and owners at all times. For instance, an in-
flated airbag triggers a phone call asking if the
driver is hurt and if so, dispatches help. Lock
your keys in the car, call OnStar to open it re-
motely. Customers even have access to the On-
Star concierge, who helps with tickets to
events, reservations, and so on.

———————— ● ————————

The world's leading speaker maker **Bose
Corporation** finds out what consumers want by
two methods: surveys and direct observation.
When the Framingham, Massachusetts–based
direct marketer conducts surveys, it doesn't
want the questions too tightly defined. Freely
asked questions illicit better answers, it finds.
Bose also watches, and films, customers installing and using its equipment to improve its
products.

———————— ● ————————

When **American Express Company** wants to
increase the venues that accept its card, it
reaches out to its cardholders. Every few
months, cardholder statements include a form
which the customers can use to tell the company about merchants they wish accepted the
card. Send it back to American Express and it

uses the card to build its base of merchants and fulfill the customer's wish at the same time.

———— • ————

In an industry that seems to reinvent itself almost every day, Rochester, New Hampshire–based **Cabletron Systems, Inc.** uses its Web site to solicit new product ideas. A maker of the hardware that connects the Internet, the $1.3 billion company uses feasibility studies to analyze the ideas and in each case, follows up with the customer.

———— • ————

Motorola, Inc. learns how customers use its products by going to work with them. In 1998, for example, workers in the $29 billion company's emergency communications products division spent a day with police officers in Chicago, Illinois. The workers not only learned how the products they make are used; they also got an indelible lesson in the critical importance of product reliability.

———— • ————

Tipton, Pennsylvania–based **New Pig Corporation** uses the ordering process to uncover customer needs. The maker and direct marketer of industrial cleaning products connected every order taker into a database nicknamed the PIT. When they get a customer comment on a product or a wish, it is dropped directly into the PIT—which is regularly mined for ideas.

"When customers call, our customer service staff is not just taking orders," explains Doug Laplante, the company's development director. "They are asking about our customers' problems. Unsolved workplace problems lead directly to new-product ideas."

———— • ————

We're always looking for new product ideas. Just call 1-800-HOT-HOGS and tell us yours.

—DOUG LAPLANTE,
NEW PIG CORPORATION

USAA (United Services Automobile Association), a financial services company for current and former military personnel, collects its customers' ideas and comments as they are offered with its ECHO system. Phone reps hit a hot key while the customer is on the phone and up pops an ECHO (Every Contact Has Opportunity) form—already completed, except for the comment itself. The reps types in the comment and sends it off to a dedicated action team. The system captures around 1,500 customer comments per week.

Is that the Maytag repairman staying at your place? **Maytag Corporation** sends ethnographers to live in selected customers' homes to find out first-hand how they live. The researchers look for patterns and Maytag translates them into new features and appliances, such as refrigerators for the car or the couch.

New Yorker magazine first reported the unique way the New York City's **Union Square Café** taps into its customers' knowledge. When it comes time to hire new staff, the restaurant solicits recommendations for servers and maitre d's from its customers. The café has received approximately 200 referrals and hired about 25 employees this way. And, whose opinion really counts when it comes to service anyway?

Retail chain **Bath & Body Works** keeps customers coming back to its line of all-natural personal care products by making sure they get to use its lotions and potions before they purchase. The stores follow a "high touch, low tech" format where employees spend their time on the floor instead of behind a cash register.

Making Complaining Easy

Stephen Tax and Stephen Brown offered these four tips to encouraging customer complaints in the *Sloan Management Review:*

1. Hire and train people for service recovery.
2. Focus service goals on fairness and customer satisfaction.
3. Remove barriers to customer complaints.
4. Track and respond to complaints.

What Are Your Value Streams?

Every business is made up of value-added processes, that consultant and author James Martin calls value streams. These are "an end-to-end collection of activities that create a result for a customer," says Martin. "The value stream has a clear goal: to satisfy or, better, to delight the customer." Identify your value streams and improve them from the customer's point of view.

─────── ● ───────

Southwest Airlines makes a point of staying close to the customer. Its Rapid Rewards frequent flyer program is modified according to customer suggestions. In the past, customers requested and received frequent flyer rewards for children and a free airline ticket for eight flights rather than 10. Much of the in-flight magazine, *Spirit*, is about Rapid Rewards programs and even its members—interviews and stories about specific members make interesting reading to other members. And all members, whether immortalized in print or not, receive greeting cards on special days including birthdays and holidays.

─────── ● ───────

Virginia newspaper **The Daily Press** knows it must connect to its readers to stay relevant and to develop the news contacts it needs. To accomplish those aims, it invites readers to its twice-daily staff meetings, weekly Editorial board meetings, and weekly News department meetings. Can't go to them? The paper will send a staff member to meet with you.

GIVE 'EM WHAT THEY WANT

Once you know what customers want, give it to them. Used to be that "out-of-print" in the book business meant out-of-luck for the customer. But now, **Simon & Schuster** is one of many publishers taking advantage of technology to eliminate out-of-print forever. It created a Demand Production Center that gives customers what they want when they want it. The high-speed printing center is already printing approximately 1.5 million "out of print" books each year in lots as small as a single copy.

Eight of ten successful new product and service ideas come from customers, says Armen Kabodian in his book, The Customer Is Always Right.

The longer a customer is retained, the more profitable he is to the firm, i.e., the fourth year a customer is an auto service company customer, the profits he generates triple over those of year one.

—JILL GRIFFIN IN *CUSTOMER LOYALTY*

———— ● ————

The **Domino's Pizza, Inc.** chain delivers their pies in expensive, new $90 warming bags made of "phase-change" material *and* it changed stores' shelving—at a cost of $4,000 per store—to fit these new bags. Why bother? To deliver a pizza to its customers that is literally hot out of the oven. In fact, the bags keep the pies at 170°, so you may even have to let it cool before eating it.

———— ● ————

The Pfaltzgraff Company makes affordable dishes that are purchased in sets. But, what happens when customers break a plate or two? Instead of forcing them to eat off mismatched plates or buy a whole new set, the company solved that customer problem with an 800 number. Call them directly to purchase individual pieces from its many sets.

———— ● ————

Customer complaints about the traditional coffee break prompted Miami, Florida–based **Hotel Inter-Continental** to offer its conference attendees a few alternatives. Among the different breaks that can be scheduled before and during meetings are "Wake Up and Stretch" workouts, "Stress Buster" sessions, and refreshments such as fruit smoothies.

———— ● ————

Fullerton, California's **Dr. Richard Hansen** addressed the unpleasantness of listening to his drill with a creative solution. His patients escape by slipping on virtual reality glasses and headphones. They can watch a movie or even a laser-like light show complete with a musical score to take their minds off the accompanying dental work.

———— ● ————

Ford Motor Company responded to its owners' desire to save their thoughts while driving with the TravelNote option now available on Explorers, Mercury Villagers, and Mountaineers. Developed by Johnson Controls, TravelNote is a digital voice recorder located in the driver's-side sun visor that holds up to three minutes of reminders, messages, and other notes. No need to hunt for pencil and paper while driving. And, it's great for cars with more than one driver. Simply leave word for the next driver to pick up that loaf of bread.

If we're not customer-driven, our cars won't be either.

—FORD MOTOR EXECUTIVE

———— • ————

Swedish carmaker **Saab Automobile AB** also innovates based on customer needs. It recently made its cars safer with a head-restraint system designed to protect against whiplash injuries in a deceptively simple way. When riders are forced into their seats as a result from impact, the seats' head restraints are automatically forced upward and forward to meet the head to avoid neck injury. And, how about keeping beverages cool? Refrigerated glove compartments prove that Saab is concerned with more than safety.

———— • ————

Japan's **Mitsubishi** gave its customers a high-tech reason to choose the Diamante model. Its Adaptive Cruise Control uses radar to automatically slow you down if you can't safely pass slower vehicles.

———— • ————

One last stop in the global car market: Germany's **BMW** now has ESP—Electronic Stability Program, that is. ESP uses yaw and pitch sensors to identify when the driver takes a curve too fast. Then, the car's onboard computer automatically makes the necessary adjustments using the braking system and the throttle.

World leader in rental cars **The Hertz Corporation** is offering customers a high-tech reason to choose them over the competition. For about $6 per day, customers can get a rental car equipped with a "NeverLost" system (a global-positioning system manufactured by Magellan under the name "PathMaster"). NeverLost is just that—the rental car helps guide its driver to a destination. A 24-satellite network determines the car's current position for an on-board computer database that directs the driver from a video screen.

People want their favorite TV programs. So, **American Airlines** added "CBS Eye on American" to its programming choices. The service offers in-flight videos of television programs from CBS, such as *60 Minutes, The Late Show with David Letterman,* and *Everybody Loves Raymond.* And, they can be viewed in either English or Spanish.

Knowing that bookstores want to reach out to their customers, but often can't afford the cost of attractive brochures, **Ingram Book Company** creates quarterly and annual glossy catalogs in several book categories, including business and religion. The catalogs are available at a very low cost and can be personalized by customers. It's a perfect solution for a company that knows that its business is dependent on its customer's business.

Retail franchiser **Wild Birds Unlimited** solved its customers' problems with storing large amounts of bird food with a simple solution. Buy as many 20- to 50-pound bags of seed during a sale and Wild Birds Unlimited will store it on their premises and track your use for free. It's a great idea that keeps bringing customers happily back to the store.

————— • —————

We highlighted **Zippo Manufacturing Company's** great guarantee (see Chapter 5); but given the decline in smoking and the rise of disposable lighters, don't you wonder how the company has survived, even prospered? The main reason is that the company watched its customers closely and learned that collectors avidly pursued its lighters. The company quickly played to the collector's market, creating limited and commemorative editions of lighters. Among the latest is the Millennium Edition lighter made from the same material as the Space Shuttle and limited to 100,000 pieces. Today, over 30% of Zippo's lighters are sold to collectors.

————— • —————

Boston, Massachusetts's **Charles Hotel** not only rewards its best customers with its Distinguished Guest Program (DGP); it also asks them what rewards they want. As a result of the effort, DGP guests no longer wait in line to check in, their rooms sport bathrobes embroidered with their names, and they get preferential seating in the hotel dining room. Exactly what they want.

————— • —————

Don't know how to properly resolve customer complaints? Deland, Florida–based wood products manufacturer **Wonderwood Corporation** simply asks customers what they want, and then gives it to them. President Ed Hurston told *Inc.* magazine that this simple strategy had reduced the cost of resolving customer complaints from about $50,000 per year to only $2,000.

————— • —————

> **The best companies are those that never stop searching for the next little thing that builds customer loyalty.**
>
> —LEONARD WOOD III,
> MARKETING DIRECTOR OF
> ROBERT E. NOLAN CO. IN
> *MANAGEMENT REVIEW*

It's easier to take an existing customer and surround him with added products than it is to go out cold turkey to someone new.

—DAVE HOLMES,
CEO OF REYNOLDS AND
REYNOLDS CO. IN
*EVERY BUSINESS
IS A GROWTH BUSINESS*

If you want to buy something, but can't find it at your local **Dillard's** department store, just see MIDD. MIDD, the Merchandise Information Desk Director, can be contacted through any Dillard's sales associate. That store's MIDD can track down any merchandise sold in the 340-plus store chain and have it sent directly to you. If the order is over $25, MIDD will even waive the shipping fees.

———— • ————

Is fitness important to you? The Beverly Hills, California–based **Hilton Hotels** chain is listening. It's currently testing specially equipped guest rooms that include items normally seen only in a gym such as workout bands, exercise bikes, exercise videos, healthy snacks, and a free copy of *Shape* magazine.

How about a stress-free environment? Hilton is also testing Stress-Less rooms. The rooms feature water peacefully gurgling from fountains, chair massagers, aromatherapy products, a special mattress, yoga tapes, and blackout curtains—at no extra charge to the customer.

———— • ————

The nation's leading food and beverage vending company **Canteen Vending Services** has responded to the public's poor perception of its goods by teaming up with respected fast-food brands, such as Blimpie's subs and Nathan's hot dogs. It plans to delight its customers with new food kiosks that stock fresh hot and cold meals made by the nationally known chains.

———— • ————

American Express knows that it has put off an entire sector of the market by requiring cardholders to pay in full every month, so it created the Extended Payment Option. Under the plan, any charge over $100 may be transferred to cardholders' American Express Optima account where it can be paid in installments. It also created the Special Purchase Account in which individual purchases of $350 or more may be paid over time.

———————— • ————————

Henrico County, Virginia's **Hampton Glen** apartments keeps its renters re-leasing by responding to their need to feel safe at home. The complex recently became the first in the state to become certified under Crime Free Multi-Housing, a program designed to "keep illegal activity out of rental property." The certification includes training, inspections by local law enforcement agencies, residents' meetings, and increased physical security— such as extra locks and deadbolts, security lighting, and door peepholes.

———————— • ————————

Want to keep customers coming back—stop hurting them! Williamsburg, Virginia's **Dr. James Burden** promises to do just that with a new high-tech MicroPrep air abrasion system that treats cavities without drills or needles. A smart development for anyone who wants to reach the estimated 100 million Americans who are dental-phobic.

———————— • ————————

Golfers are always bragging about distance, but who's to say exactly how many yards that ball flew? Now, at **Ford's Colony,** a residential resort community boasting a couple of popular public golf courses in Virginia, your golf cart will tell you. Ford's Colony is one of an estimated 200 courses in the country that offer electronic yardage monitors in every golf cart.

Ever wonder why the cool stuff never gets to the coach seats? Thirty-seven percent of airline revenues come from the high-mileage business travelers—just six percent of passengers.

The systems, that work using global positioning equipment, also allow for emergency communications, message retrieval, and even food order placement.

———— • ————

UAL Corporation's United Airlines addresses noise pollution inside its planes with the Noisebuster system. Currently in use in first- and business-class service, the system uses noise cancellation headsets to eliminate the roar of the jet engines and make listening to movies and music on board a more pleasant experience.

———— • ————

American Airlines' new Boeing 777s give new meaning to flying First Class with a fully reclining, flat sleeper seat with its own privacy divider. Each seat pair also has a second divider screen and all the usual amenities such as satellite phones, personal video/audio entertainment systems, adjustable lumbar support, and individual power ports.

———— • ————

Delta Air Lines put its efforts into a new BusinessElite service. It is all about personal space with seats that offer "52% more legroom than British Airways and 28° more recline than American Airlines." In addition, with only two seats on either side, no BusinessElite flyer has to sit in the dreaded middle seat. BusinessElite also offers a higher flight attendant to passenger ratio and five-course dining served with award-winning wines.

———— • ————

Our favorite, however, is **Alitalia's** new *Magnifica* Class. It's got leather-trimmed reclining seats, award-winning meals, and chauffeur-driven transfers upon landing in Rome and Milan. But, it's probably just the name that hooked us.

———— ❦ ————

Maybe some cool stuff does reach the back of the plane: **Virgin Atlantic Airways** is giving every passenger his or her own video screen on its transatlantic flights. The screen is located on the seat back in front of the passenger and comes with its own remote control for easy operation. Passengers can choose from movies, television, and even, video games.

———— ❦ ————

New York–based **OmniGuard** created a business that answers the art collector's most persistent worry—authenticity. OmniGuard offers a database and a tamper-proof mark complete with unique identification number that is affixed to a new work of art when it is made. Not only can buyers be sure that the work is authentic; it also eliminates the possibility of forgery.

———— ❦ ————

Many people want to commute by bicycle, but don't have the energy to make it from here to there and back without some help. And, that's where Sebastopol, California–based **ZAP!** got the idea for its electric-powered bicycles. ZAP! (which stands for Zero Air Pollution) manufactures electric bicycles and conversion packs for standard bikes. Both look like normal bikes except for a small battery pack near the front wheel. In a time when fitness is king but the population is aging, ZAP! gives riders the choice to pedal under their own power or use the bike's power pack to motor at up to 14 mph for about 14 miles.

———— ❦ ————

Even staid clothier **Brooks Brothers** is acting on the voice of the customer these days. Well-known for suits, trousers, blazers, and even casuals in stately fabrics and time-proven designs, the company is introducing bright new

> No matter what business you're in, your customers all want the same three things: They want it *free,* they want it *perfect,* and they want it *now.*
>
> —ROB RODIN, CEO OF MARSHALL INDUSTRIES

> Anything that won't sell, I don't want to invent. Its sale is proof of utility, and utility is success.
>
> —THOMAS ALVA EDISON

colors and has gone as far as installing an espresso bar in its Madison Avenue, New York City store. Gasp!

————— ● —————

Sometimes, what customers want is the best price they can get. The Topeka, Kansas–based **Newcomer Family Funeral Homes, Inc.** chain is expanding fast by pioneering the discount funeral. With the average funeral in 1996 costing upwards of $4,782, a Newcomer funeral averages only $2,585. And, it's telling customers about it with TV advertising—another break with tradition.

————— ● —————

Seattle-based **Pro Air** is competing on price against the major airlines. It took wing in the Detroit market after determining that the prices there were among the highest in the country for air travel. And, it is grabbing market share by beating the competition by as much as $582 per flight, according to *Inc.* magazine.

————— ● —————

If you plan to compete on price, cyberspace may be the best place to set up business. Virginia-based **Telebank, Inc.** has no branches, no ATMs, no sites at all—except its headquarters. It is set up on the direct-to-customer model and as a result, its costs are less than half the typical bank. So what? The cost savings are passed on to customers in higher savings rates and lower fees.

————— ● —————

Here's a nice one: **Land's End** established the Lost Mitten Club for its young customers, who are prone to, that's right, losing their mittens. If your kids lose a Land's End mitten during the same season you bought it, the company will sell you one mitten—at half the price of the pair—and ship it free.

PERSONALIZE IT

Here is a worthy challenge: Make every customer feel like you create products and services designed specifically for them. **Levi Strauss & Company** does. Using computer technology in stores, consumers can design their own Levi's jeans. Customers choose their preferred style options and their measurements are taken and entered into the system. The company then makes and ships a pair of pants that perfectly fit the customer.

———— ◦ ————

Here's a couple of simpler ones to implement: **Boston Proper** women's clothing cataloger helps customers get the right fit by starting with their measurements. Customers take their own measurements, call Boston Proper, and customer service representatives help choose the proper garments and sizes based on their clients' actual size.

———— ◦ ————

Catalog retailer **Norm Thompson** offers a little customization of its own. Customers buying pants get them hemmed to fit at no additional charge—they need only supply their finished inseam. A perfect fit without leaving the house.

———— ◦ ————

Why not ask customers when they want their bill? **Chase Manhattan** offers the "Billing Preference Option" on its Cashbuilder Gold Visa Card. Customers decide whether to have their payments due in the beginning, middle, or end of the month to best fit into their own cash-flow cycle.

———— ◦ ————

Forget about sifting through stacks of brochures for your next cruise and check out

We are about to see extraordinary levels of erosion in customer loyalty, a trend that will get worse before it gets better. Only companies that interact with, learn from, and personalize their products and services for their customers . . . stand a chance of weathering the customer free-for-all that lies ahead.

—DON PEPPERS IN *INSIDE 1TO1*

American Express Travel's online "Cruise Assist" feature. Complete a survey of preferences and priorities and Cruise Assist identifies the perfect cruise or vacation for you.

American Express also customizes every cardholder statement with personalized promotions and specials. Known as CustomExtras, the program offers discounts, upgrades, and gifts based on the past purchases of the cardholder.

American Express is even customizing its free incentive gifts. Register to use American Express Online Services, a fee-free service itself, and American Express gives you a free one-year subscription to the magazine of your choice, picked from over 300 possibilities.

———— ● ————

Department store shoppers got the same privilege during a recent **Elizabeth Arden** cosmetics promotion. They were invited to choose their own five free goodies with any purchase of $18.50 from among eight products, including lipstick, perfume, mascara, eye shadow, and other items, and take them all home in a free cosmetic bag. It's always better to give customers what they want.

———— ● ————

General Motor's Pontiac division keeps in touch with its customers with a free magazine specifically suited to their lifestyle, model year, brand of car, and location. It is also customized for the selling dealer, who puts a letter and specifically targeted coupons in each issue.

———— ● ————

Chicago-based **Northwestern Medical Faculty Foundation** uses a similar strategy by personalizing and customizing their "Health Notes" newsletter. It uses patient histories and profiles to determine the individualized content and a new issue is sent with each monthly bill.

———— • ————

Home Depot takes the customized newsletter a step further by electrifying it. Sign up for its e-mailed HomeMinder service and the do-it-yourself chain will deliver yard and home maintenance news developed specifically for your region.

———— • ————

The Ohio-based **Dorothy Lane** grocery chain tracks the buying patterns of its Club DLM customers and uses the information to target its promotional mailings. Customers receive customized packets of coupons and other offers that are related to the products they already use.

———— • ————

ATM's not easy enough? The UK's **Natwest Bank** lets customers personalize them. Clients set up their preferences in advance—a regular withdrawal amount, for instance—and input the information once. After that, they choose the Personal Option button at the bank's ATM and the rest is automatic.

———— • ————

Capital Concierge applies the personal service provided by the hotel concierge to the corporate office. It places its employees inside its corporate clients' offices and links them to a proprietary software network to keep them in the know. The concierges provide services including dining reservations, sports and entertainment tickets, golf tee times, valet services, catering, and more. They also remind customers of birthdays, anniversaries, and other special events, and handle any gift or get-together arrangements for these dates.

Revolve your world around the customer and more customers will revolve around you.

—HEATHER WILLIAMS

————— ● —————

On the gruesome side: Coral Gables, Florida dermatologist **Fredric Brandt** keeps customers coming back after cosmetic surgery by storing removed tissue at BioBank, a Beverly, Massachusetts, "biological safety deposit box." The tissue is processed down to collagen and elastin and can be reused by the same patients for "autologen" treatments. Since it is only used by the patient it originally belonged to, the patient knows exactly what he or she is getting and the body will not reject it.

————— ● —————

Who's that photographing your clothes? *Inside 1to1* reports that it is Connecticut clothing store **Mitchells of Westport.** Mitchell photographs its customer's purchases, creating a photo album of sorts. The sales staff matches new merchandise to the album and notifies their clients of its availability.

————— ● —————

CNN revolutionized television news with 24-hour coverage. Now, they have expanded their online service by offering personalized news. At CNN Interactive, customers choose from over 2,000 topics in 300 categories to personalize their news retrieval. CNN updates the site every 15 minutes and runs over 20,000 news stories each week.

————— ● —————

The Digital Era is personalizing the music business, too. **CDuctive** is an online music retailer that allows customers to create their own CDs. Choose the music you like from any of the over 50 independent record labels CDuctive is licensed to sell, preview the tracks by listening to 45-second samples, and click to create your customized CD.

———— ◈ ————

Great ideas attract competition, so look for personal CDs online at **The Music Connection,** too. You can even personalize the CD cover art and text, and use "The Music Advisor" feature that will make suggestions based on your prior purchases and the choices of other customers with similar taste.

———— ◈ ————

Amazon.com also makes suggestions based on individual customer preferences. The site's BookMatcher feature tracks buying history and areas of interest to recommend additional titles; MoodMatcher does the same using "more subjective criteria," such as other reader's purchases. Add in the site's 1-Click ordering system that remembers previous purchase information, and you've got a tough package to beat.

Why stop at just books? With the launch of its online auction service, Amazon.com added another twist to its recommendation tools. Search for a book, and when it pops up so does a sidebar with related items available on the auction. For example, an art catalog of Peter Max prints may bring up the prints themselves available for sale on the auction site.

———— ◈ ————

Forget about those cheesy, stock icing designs for your next birthday cake. Bring a personal photo, company graphic, or any other scanned image to select **Farm Fresh** supermarkets and for about the cost of a traditionally decorated cake, the store will make a sheet cake, large cookie, or cupcake topped with the image in edible icing. The secret of the pilot program: a digital image that is airbrushed onto a cake using food coloring instead of ink.

———— ◈ ————

Bausch & Lomb, Inc.'s perennially cool Ray-Ban sunglasses come in over 150 styles and used to require a trip to the store to preview. Forget about that, dudes. Now mail your picture to the company, and they will scan it and give you a password to view yourself at www.rayban.com. Drop in from your desk and try 'em on to your heart's content.

———— ● ————

The possibilities of digital imaging don't stop there. **Acclaimed Appearance** salon uses a digital camera and computer monitor to let clients "try on" new hair styles and colors before making any changes. Clients review hundreds of hairstyles, choose those they are interested in, and get to see themselves in the new style and/or hair color on the monitor.

———— ● ————

Local favorite **Cooke's Garden Center** doesn't just promise you a rose garden. They will show how the garden will look in your yard before spade hits soil. Owner Jeff Schell photographs the site and with his computer, "places" the specified items in the yard. Color printing rounds out the service.

———— ● ————

Kids hate the taste of medicine. At least they used to. At **Ukrop's Super Market,** the pharmacist will fix that at the parent's request. They offer a host of flavorings, including bubble gum, butterscotch, cherry, chocolate, peppermint, coconut, or other childhood favorites.

———— ● ————

In the better-living-through-chemistry department: **Acumin,** an online seller of vitamins, will make daily vitamin tablets configured just for you. Customers complete a questionnaire including age, stress levels, dietary concerns,

Everything starts with the customer.

—Source Unknown

and activity levels; and Acumin produces a pill formula created for their specific needs.

———— ● ————

Bloomingdale's "At His Service" program offers many services, including a personal shopper at no charge. Designed especially for the non-shopper (read that "male of the species"), At His Service clients simply e-mail the store stating what type of shopping they need done. An At His Service shopper collects and presents the choices in any number of convenient locations, including a private area in the store or the client's home or office. After the items are chosen, At His Service completes the sale with gift wrap, delivery, alterations, and so on. Provide a list of your dates to remember and you get a reminder call in plenty of time to make the necessary arrangements.

———— ● ————

San Francisco–based **Sharper Image Corporation** has a department dedicated to helping its corporate customers create reward programs for their own employees. The $200 million company's corporate incentive professionals run the accounts from planning to fulfillment. And, they offer options such as personalized Sharper Image Merchandise Certificates redeemable for products in Sharper Image stores, catalogs or online, and volume discounts on specific reward items.

———— ● ————

Godiva Chocolatier will happily take over your entire corporate gift-giving program. The company handles the individual deliveries throughout the U.S., adds your business card or a personalized message ribbon with your logo to each gift, and discounts your order for its trouble. Corporate discounts run from 5%

Customize, customize, customize. It is the great differentiator of the twenty-first century.

—STAN DAVIS & CHRISTOPHER MEYER IN *BLUR*

for orders of $500 and up to 20% for orders of $3,000.

———— • ————

Direct computer giant **Dell Computer Corporation** built its business on the have-it-your-way computer. Customers call a customer rep or log on to the PC makers' hugely popular Web site, decide exactly what configuration best suits their needs, and in around five days, their custom PC is sitting at their door.

Not surprisingly, this ease of service, and the cost advantages that go with it, has made Dell a favorite among corporate buyers also. The company even sets up personalized product and support mini-Web sites for its larger corporate customers. The Premier Pages program allows the customers to post their pre-approved product configurations, purchase orders, and pricing. It also lets big customers track orders and inventory and contact Dell's account and support staff. Premier Pages makes the boundaries between customer and vendor more transparent than ever.

———— • ————

There is nothing rote about Calgary, Alberta–based **Smed International, Inc.** The office systems maker even creates customized plant tours. Touring customers can see the entire facility or follow a product line or simply try out the chairs, desks, cabinets, and workspace configurations. Clients are also offered concierge services and private offices during their visit, along with access to a computer program with complete product details. CEO Mogans Smed told *Inc.*, "[The customer's] time is worth about 10 times our cost."

———— • ————

Midwest Express Airlines offers personalized online services to its frequent flyers. They may store a member profile online that remembers details including contact information, credit card numbers, seating preference, meal service requirements, and origination/destination airports. Members booking flights online do not need to re-enter any of this information; it is automatically retrieved and used when needed. Members can also get quotes, and check their air miles and the status of flights.

————— ● —————

Jiffy Lube is where everyone knows your name. The company's customer database allows employees to enter your license plate number and access your name and service history in an instant. Add a small fee and the quick oil change experts will sign you up for Signature Service, which recommends services based on information from your vehicle's manufacturer.

————— ● —————

Faced with a rapidly shrinking customer base, **Deere & Company,** the world's largest farm equipment maker, turned to mass customization to drive sales. When customers want their Deere equipment to perform new tasks, a team at the factory will go to work creating a one-of-a-kind attachment to solve the problem. The customer gets added value without replacing the entire machine, and Deere keeps its factories busy and its coffers full.

————— ● —————

Holland, Michigan–based **Haworth, Inc.** applied have-it-your-way to its office furniture business. The sales force is happy to team up with customers to alter existing designs or create new ones. They have a software program that gives clients a visual image of what they've created and allows changes in style, color, or size on the spot. Once approved by the clients, the computer generates the plan and Haworth goes to work.

It's no trick to be a successful salesman if you have what people want. You never hear bootleggers complaining about hard times.

—Humorist Robert Edwards

11

BECOME A CUSTOMER SERVICE CHAMP

Ultimately, the success of all of the great programs and incentives and services you create to keep your customers coming back boils down to the ability to deliver them. Since that delivery is the job of your company's employees, the challenge of customer retention comes down to the people working in your company.

To be successful, your company has to be focused on customers from the top down and from the outside in. Every time an employee encounters a customer, that corporate focus is tested and an opportunity to build the loyalty bond occurs.

An intense customer focus starts with the boss. The leaders of a business are the most influential models for its employees. If all they care about is this month's bottom line, that is exactly what employees will try to increase—at whatever the cost. If, however, the customer is a leader's primary concern, the foundation of a customer service champion is laid.

With a foundation in place, a company must support the customer focus with a specially tailored infrastructure. Training, systems, and compensation must be aligned with intent. Mixed messages must be eliminated. Companies can't pay telephone reps a bonus based on

Three Steps for Turning Your Customers into Raving Fans

Here's the process Ken Blanchard and Sheldon Bowles teach in their book, *Raving Fans:*

1. Create a corporate vision of perfection.

2. Ask customers what they want and build those needs into your vision.

3. Deliver and continuously improve the vision.

how many phone calls they complete and expect them not to rush customers.

And, finally, companies must regularly reinforce the customer focus. They need to celebrate customer service. They need to motivate and reward great customer service. This is what we try to do in the final section of this chapter—leave you with ideas and examples that excite your best efforts to keep customers coming back.

CUSTOMER RETENTION STARTS AT THE TOP

One of the best ways to achieve customer satisfaction is by successfully resolving a customer complaint. **AlliedSignal** knows it cannot always satisfy the customer on the first try because of demands unique to the aerospace industry. But when an AlliedSignal customer complains, it goes to CEO Larry Bossidy, who calls or visits the customer himself. Bossidy wants to learn the nature of the complaint first-hand so that it may be resolved quickly. The CEO also insists that AlliedSignal employees tell customers the whole truth on delivery schedules and product progress, even if the truth is bad news.

———— ● ————

Southwest Airlines founder and CEO Herb Kelleher keeps employees motivated to provide exemplary customer service by showing them the way. For example, upon learning that an entire class of Dallas students had never had the opportunity to fly in an airplane, Kelleher sent them all free roundtrip tickets to Austin and even threw in a guided tour of the Texas Capital.

Each year at Thanksgiving, notoriously one of the heaviest airline travel days of the year, Kelleher shows up at the airport and does an honest day's work with Southwest's ground crews in Dallas. This is no cakewalk for the CEO—Southwest's planes are refueled, unloaded, reloaded, cleaned, and restocked in only 20 minutes or about half the time it takes most other airlines.

———— ● ————

Transportation and logistics provider **Continental Traffic Service, Inc.** gets closer to its customers by learning all it can about them. CEO Kenneth Hazen purchases one share of any publicly traded customer stock as a way to keep track of his customers' plans and objectives through their annual reports and corporate communications. Each share of stock is also framed and provides the company's front foyer decorations. Hazen says it impresses the customers and helps to remind even those employees who never meet the company's customers of exactly who their real customers are.

———— ● ————

Service championship starts at the top. **America Online** president & COO Bob Pittman regularly puts himself in his customer's shoes by refusing in-house training on product and service enhancements. Instead, he goes to his computer and attempts to utilize the new service as any of his online subscribers might. Pittman knows if he can't figure it out himself, AOL customers will probably have a hard time too.

———— ● ————

Michael Dell, the founder and CEO of **Dell Computer Corporation,** also knows the customer is king. Twice each year, he chairs Platinum Council meetings, which are held in various

Customer service now has its own MBA program at University of Texas at Austin's Graduate School of Business. Graduates of The Center for Customer Insight's program are trained to build great customer service programs.

Values-driven leaders infuse their values into the fabric of the organization. They lead not with commands, not with a thick rule book, but with a set of core values—what the firm represents and aspires to be.

—Leonard Berry, professor at Texas A&M University in his book, *Discovering the Soul of Service*

regions around the world. In these meetings, upper management sits down with customers to learn about their needs, concerns, and visions for the future. All of this shared information helps Dell lead the company in directions that will benefit customers.

The company's systems also support a customer focus. Both the employee profit-sharing and incentive-compensation plans are tied to measurable customer satisfaction data.

———⬤———

Unisys Corporation CEO James Unruh wrote the book on customer service. Well, one of them at least, *Customers Mean Business* (Addison-Wesley, 1996). His main lesson is that great service starts with listening. Unruh says he spends half his time on the road and a majority of that face-to-face with customers. The results are two-fold: the fact that the CEO is listening leaves no doubt about the company's commitment to customers; and, the information gathered determines the company's future strategies.

———⬤———

Subway Sandwich Shops, Inc. founder Fred Deluca gets a customer's-eye view of his company's 13,000 plus franchises with regular road trips. He picks a region and spends a week or two visiting shops—without announcing the visit or identifying himself. "This way, I'm able to get a firsthand feel about what's going on," he explains in *Predatory Marketing*. "I travel with a tape recorder, and in between stops, I record my thoughts. I always come home with tapes filled with ideas on improvements we could make—from a customer's point of view."

———⬤———

A great story about customer service commitment at the top: When **The Home Depot** chain first started expanding, growth outpaced service and customer service became a serious issue. To build corporate focus, the senior management created an imaginary director of consumer affairs by the name of Ben Hill. In each store, they prominently posted Ben Hill's name and his 800#, asking customers to call if they had any problems.

"The number went into our main office switchboard in Atlanta. Whenever somebody called it and asked to speak to Ben Hill, we didn't ask, 'What is it regarding?' The name 'Ben Hill' was code red for 'Expedite the call *right now*.' The call would be directed to Arthur, Pat, me, or whoever was the highest-ranking person in the company available at the time of the call," remembers founder Bernie Marcus in *Built from Scratch*. "It didn't matter if we were signing a million-dollar deal; we stopped and took the call. We wanted our customers to get to the right people and get their problem solved."

Even better, when the staff at the stores realized who Ben Hill was, customer satisfaction complaints plummeted.

> Our philosophy of customer service is "Whatever it takes." That means we'll do whatever it takes to satisfy a customer within all human reason.
>
> —BERNIE MARCUS
> AND ARTHUR BLANK,
> FOUNDERS OF HOME DEPOT

BUILD YOUR BUSINESS AROUND THE CUSTOMER

You can't find out what customers think if you never meet them. **The Timken Company,** a Bucyrus, Ohio steelmaker, hosts monthly visitor days for its customers. Customers are invited to presentations, shop-floor demonstrations and luncheon discussions. All levels of Timken employees participate, giving customers direct access to both decision-makers and the folks who make the products.

———————●———————

Southwest Airlines makes sure it teaches its employees to keep customers coming back.

> **No employee will ever be punished for using good judgment and good old common sense when trying to accommodate a customer, no matter what our other rules are."**
>
> —SOUTHWEST AIRLINES
> CUSTOMER SERVICE POLICY

The company requires courses such as "Customer Care" and runs periodic seminars and workshops on the topic. They also learn by example because Southwest believes that employees will treat customers the same way they themselves are treated. Apparently, customers agree and keep coming back because Southwest consistently earns the status of being the best airline in terms of on-time performance, baggage handling, and customer satisfaction.

———— ● ————

Rosenbluth International hones its employees' customer skills with a training program named Client Retention and Development. This three-day training seminar is completed by about 250 employees each year. It teaches relationship building, listening, customer perspective, and proactive problem solving.

———— ● ————

Coeur d'Alene–based direct marketer **Coldwater Creek** lets customers know, "We Work Hard to Make Shopping Easy." It answers catalog calls in an average of five seconds—not with a recording, but by a trained company representative. To make sure customer questions are answered quickly and without transfers, the phone centers have a sample of each catalog item on hand. Reps are encouraged to wear the company's clothing, jewelry, and accessories so they can speak from experience. Their secret: operators who are "just naturally friendly and helpful."

———— ● ————

Ukrop's supermarkets wants its customers to complain—that is, if they are unhappy. The company keeps a toll-free customer-service line available to all shoppers, regardless of which store they frequent.

More unusual is the fact that Ukrop's re-contacts unhappy customers after a month to make sure their problem was resolved. We were privy to one follow-up where the customer had not been fully satisfied. This time, the company sent a $20 store gift certificate and a warm "thank you for your business" note to further solve a problem—which originally involved an incorrect charge of less than $2.

————————— ● —————————

Luxury is as luxury does: The **RIHGA Royal Hotel** in New York City is an all-suite luxury hotel catering to the business community, especially communications and entertainment celebrities, that has made customer service championship a daily occurrence. The top 25 floors of the 54-story hotel are reserved for the best of the best, known as Pinnacle Suites. Pinnacle Suites come equipped with private phone lines, in-room fax machines and private fax lines, voice mail, and in-room and limousine cell phones.

But maybe the real reason high-powered executives keep coming back to the RHIGA's Pinnacle Suites is the business cards. Guests checking in to the hotel receive a leather case containing personalized business cards with their name and all their private RHIGA phone numbers on it. The cards show off the RHIGA name and state that the guest is "In Residence" and even include the scheduled departure date.

————————— ● —————————

The service accorded guests at the private villas at California's posh **Peninsula Beverly Hills** rivals RHIGA. It costs a king's ransom to stay, but the staff maintains an "Absence of Discomfort" policy for the guests. There is no check-in or checkout time. The hotel accommodates busy schedules by providing complete freedom

> To win the devotion of customers, leaders must build an organization worthy of that devotion. You cannot win the hearts of customers unless you have a heart yourself.
>
> —CHARLOTTE BEERS IN
> *LEADER TO LEADER*

The Strategic Planning Institute found that companies that placed great emphasis on customer service earned 12 times the return on sales of those that did not stress customer service.

to come and go as their guests' schedules allow. Regulars' preferences are kept on file so that they find customized extras upon their return to the hotel, such as monogrammed designer bathrobes and towels along with personalized "in residence" stationery. The hotel will even move furniture in and/or out of the rooms according to their guests' lifestyle. And, there are several employees available at all hours such as spa attendants, concierges, bell staff, and management to handle their guests' requests, problems and, of course, whims.

———————————●———————————

Examples of **Nordstrom, Inc.'s** dazzling customer service abound. One of our favorites is a simple one that speaks volumes: A shopper we know hit a New Jersey mall late one day. He tried to enter one department store, but was turned away. He headed for Nordstrom's, where a salesperson greeted him this way: "Hi, we're closing. Come on in."

Now a frequent Nordstrom customer, this same customer is particularly dazzled by his personal shopper. He calls, talks about what he wants, and makes an appointment. When he arrives at the store, pre-selected clothing is hanging in the dressing room for him to try on.

It's not just attitude. Nordstrom's maintains a clerk-to-customer ratio that is three times higher than the industry average. And, it trains and trusts those employees to do the right thing. As for rules, the now-legendary employee handbook has only one: "Use good judgment in all situations."

———————————●———————————

Great service businesses empower their employees to solve problems. Baldrige Award winner **Zytec Corporation** makes sure its employees have the tools they need to keep customers coming back. The Redwood Falls, Minnesota electronic power supply manufacturer trains all its employee using the *Service America* program and, once trained, each of the company's employees is empowered to spend up to $1,000 to immediately solve service problems.

———— • ————

At **The Ritz-Carlton Hotel Company,** empowerment means every employee is authorized to spend up to $2,000 to resolve a complaint from a guest. Most of the time, that kind of investment is not required, but when employees know their company is that serious about solving problems, problems get solved.

———— • ————

You get what you measure. When a customer complains at **Charles Schwab & Company, Inc.,** the discount brokerage does more than track the complaint. To get a true reading on how well the complaint was resolved, Schwab measures how much business the complaining customer does with the company in the next six months.

———— • ————

You also get what you pay for. Sales automation software developer **Siebel Systems** makes sure its employees realize exactly how important its customers are by basing employee bonuses on customer satisfaction. Customer satisfaction levels are measured quarterly by outside auditors.

———— • ————

Pitney Bowes helps its sales force to focus on more than just the sale with its bonus system. The bonuses are tied to meeting or exceeding customer satisfaction targets after the sale. Some of the company's measures: how thoroughly the

> **Nordstrom believes in "hiring the smile and training the skill." I once asked then-co-chairman Bruce Nordstrom who trains his salespeople, and he answered: "Their parents."**
>
> **—Robert Spector in *Customer Service***

customer is trained, how well the equipment was installed, and degree of support.

CELEBRATE CUSTOMER CHAMPIONS

Middleton, Wisconsin's **WinterSilks** won the 1996 Direct Marketing Association Award for Customer Service Excellence. How did it get to the top? Fixed operational goals, including answering calls within 16 seconds, same-day resolution on customer complaints, 99.5% accuracy on orders shipped, and at least 80% of all orders shipped the same day.

———— • ————

Join the **International Customer Service Association** (www.isca.com). The Chicago-based professional association sponsors the newly established SOUL (Service On Unbelievable Levels) Awards and a certification program for customer service pros, as well as conferences, publications, and regional activities.

———— • ————

Marriott International, Inc. celebrates service excellence among its employees with annual awards. The Tiefel Award, established in 1989, recognizes "extraordinary service rendered by associates to guests and, on occasion, to one another," according to CEO J. W. Marriott, Jr. The hotel chain also presents the J. Willard Marriott Award of Excellence to employees who regularly bring to life the company's service values.

———— • ————

How did Victoria Gallegos sell $2 million worth of designer goods and become 1998 Salesperson of the Year in the **Prada** retail chain? Gallegos told the *New Yorker* that she:

- Ignores financial goals, concentrating instead on relationships.
- Pays attention to her clients, sending holiday notes, birthday cakes, and making sickroom visits.
- Welcomes visits from customers—sometimes to buy, sometimes to talk, sometimes to discuss their latest purchases from other stores and boutiques.
- Spends time in Prada's stockrooms and with buyers to learn about the materials and product lines.
- Pampers shoppers with soft drinks and cookies she brings to work herself.
- Encloses a personalized thank-you note in every order.
- Is always available—clients have her home, work, and beeper numbers.

—————— • ——————

Customer service is a mindset and it exists wherever people care. An eyeglass wearer who happened into **Dr. Carter L. Murphy's** Williamsburg office after the arm of a five-year old pair of glasses fell off reported this story. Even though the pair was not purchased there and the wearer was not a client, the staff searched the office for 15 minutes to locate the replacement parts and fixed the glasses without charge for time or parts. They could not have known they were earning a customer for life.

—————— • ——————

When you really want to learn about superlative service, hotel concierges are the ones to watch. *The Washington Post* recently celebrated three: The Reston, Virginia **Hyatt Regency's** concierge Susan Drosdzal went above and beyond the call of duty by literally outfitting a guest for a job interview after her luggage was lost.

> **The central business issue should be how to meet the needs of a group of people in a way that is fulfilling for employees, satisfying for customers, profitable for shareholders, and responsible for the community.**
>
> —MARK ALBION,
> BUSINESS WRITER

Motivate them, train them, care about them, and make winners out of them. If we treat our employees correctly, they'll treat the customers right. And if the customers are treated right, they'll come back.

—J. W. MARRIOTT, JR.

———— ● ————

At the **Ritz-Carlton** in Chicago, Chief Concierge John Winke is famous for service, including the replacement of lost contact lenses for the mother of a bride—just two hours before the wedding, and bringing in a rocking chair from his home so that a baby could be rocked to sleep.

———— ● ————

Not willing to be outdone, **The Four Seasons Hotel** in Chicago boasts general manager Hans Willimann, who after surveying a room full of guests awaiting the arrival of former President and Mrs. Reagan, found a lone guest without a tuxedo. Willimann quickly arranged for the use and proper fitting of an employee's tuxedo, and the guest was back among his peers without missing a beat. The guest turned out to be the CEO of a management consulting company, now a loyal customer.

———— ● ————

A good rebuttal to the typical Hollywood portrayal of greedy insurance companies is this story about **The Northwestern Mutual Life Insurance Company,** told in *Good Company:* When a student pilot died in a crash during training (an exclusionary period on his insurance policy), his family assumed they would receive no benefits. When his logbook was recovered, however, Northwestern discovered that he had reached the 100 hours required to become a standard risk on his final flight. His family received the full benefit.

———— ● ————

Brag about your commitment to service; it's a good thing. **Land's End,** the clothing cataloger, created a wonderful ad campaign using the thank-you letters they receive from their customers for going above and beyond the call of duty. One featured a child's parka that was returned to Land's End from Tokyo. When employees found the former owner's toy monster in the pocket, they returned the toy to its rightful owner.

In another example, a German customer ordered a tie and asked for instructions on how to tie it. The Land's End employee who sent the tie did one better—the employee sent along another complimentary tie, already knotted as well as the instructions.

And, from England, a heavily used attaché case was returned to Land's End requesting a broken zipper repair. Land's End sent out a new one, for free. Exemplary customer service goes a long way toward building a loyal clientele. And there is no reason why you shouldn't spread the word yourself.

———————●———————

Celebrate **National Customer Service Week!** Created by the International Customer Service Association in 1988 and made official by the U.S. Congress in 1992, is a good time to intensify the corporate focus on service, recognize your customer service champs, and thank customers. National Customer Service Week is the first full business week in October.

Houston-based **BMC Software, Inc.** did. The data management software maker partied with a quirky fiesta that featured jalapeño-spitting and limbo contests, and golf, basketball, and darts—all at the office. Amid all the fun, the company also hosted customer service sessions for the staff and local businesses.

> The magic formula that successful businesses have discovered is to treat customers like guests and employees like people.
>
> —Tom Peters

INDEX